Measuring Intelligence

D0217255

The testing of intelligence has a long and controversial history. Claims that it is a pseudo-science or a weapon of ideological warfare have been commonplace and there is not even a consensus as to whether intelligence exists and, if it does, whether it can be measured. As a result the debate about it has centred on the nurture versus nature controversy and especially on alleged racial differences and the heritability of intelligence – all of which have major policy implications. This book aims to penetrate the mists of controversy, ideology and prejudice by providing a clear non-mathematical framework for the definition and measurement of intelligence derived from modern factor analysis. Building on this framework and drawing on everyday ideas the author addresses key controversies in a clear and accessible style and explores some of the claims made by well-known writers in the field such as Stephen Jay Gould and Michael Howe.

DAVID J. BARTHOLOMEW is Emeritus Professor of Statistics, London School of Economics, Fellow of the British Academy and a former president of the Royal Statistical Society. He is a member of the editorial board of various journals and has published numerous books and journal articles in the fields of statistics and social measurement.

Measuring Intelligence

Facts and Fallacies

David J. Bartholomew

London School of Economics and Political Science

PUBLISHED BY THE PRESS SYNDICATE OF THE UNIVERSITY OF CAMBRIDGE
The Pitt Building, Trumpington Street, Cambridge, United Kingdom

CAMBRIDGE UNIVERSITY PRESS
The Edinburgh Building, Cambridge, CB2 2RU, UK
40 West 20th Street, New York, NY 10011–4211, USA
477 Williamstown Road, Port Melbourne, VIC 3207, Australia
Ruiz de Alarcón 13, 28014 Madrid, Spain
Dock House, The Waterfront, Cape Town 8001, South Africa

http://www.cambridge.org

© David J. Bartholomew 2004

This book is in copyright. Subject to statutory exception
and to the provisions of relevant collective licensing agreements,
no reproduction of any part may take place without
the written permission of Cambridge University Press.

First published 2004

Printed in the United Kingdom at the University Press, Cambridge

Typeface Times 10/12 pt.   *System* LATEX 2$_\varepsilon$ [TB]

A catalogue record for this book is available from the British Library

ISBN 0 521 83619 0 hardback
ISBN 0 521 54478 5 paperback

The publisher has used its best endeavours to ensure that the URLs for external
websites referred to in this book are correct and active at the time of going to press.
However, the publisher has no responsibility for the websites and can make no
guarantee that a site will remain live or that the content is or will remain appropriate.

Contents

Full contents

Figures

Preface

Human intelligence is one of the most important yet controversial topics in the whole field of the human sciences. It is not even agreed whether it can be measured or, if it can, whether it should be measured. The literature is enormous and much of it is highly partisan and, often, far from accurate.

To justify a further incursion into this field it may help to think of the sporting analogy provided by professional football, of whatever code. There are many people who take a passing interest in the game; they may look up scores in the newspaper, but have little specialist interest and they would certainly not feel deprived if they were cut off from the game altogether. Then there are those we may call spectators, who follow the game closely. They may attend matches and watch games on television. Some will be violently partisan, cheering on their own team, failing to see the fouls on their opponents and hurling occasional abuse at the referee. Others will be connoisseurs who understand the niceties of the game and delight in the skills and artistry of the players. Only a few people will actually be engaged in the game as players. They are the ones who have a good technical knowledge of the rules but, more importantly, have the outstanding skills which enable them to perform well at the professional level. For them it is more than just a game, it is also the source of their livelihood. Finally, there are one or more referees, by whatever name, whose job is to see that the game is played according to the rules without advantage to either side.

This book is written from the referee's point of view. Although many people take a general interest in intelligence testing and research, it plays no significant part in their lives. Fewer, whom we might call the spectators, take a close interest in what is happening, perhaps because it is relevant to their work. Some will be firm supporters of the pro- or anti-factions. Others will try to take a balanced view, acquainting themselves with the latest research. All will benefit from the fact that the spectator often sees more of the game. Neither group, nor the many in between, have the first hand acquaintance with the game which can only come from being a player. There are many books written by players for spectators and yet more by spectators for other spectators, and also for that much larger group who take a passing interest. The referee, however, is the expert on the rules and, although that role may be less glamorous, the livelihood of the players and the enjoyment of the spectators depends upon the job being done properly. The referee's view is much needed in the literature of the intelligence game and this book aims to provide it.

Measuring intelligence is no simple matter. If it were, the principal arguments would have been settled long ago. Measurement involves numbers and numeracy is not one of the strengths of contemporary culture. The aim of this book is to express quantitative ideas in words and the occasional diagram. This needs patience on the part of the reader and a willingness to give the material the detailed attention which it requires.

It is a sad fact that many of those who have written on the subject, especially in a polemical vein, have failed to fully understand the technicalities of the subject. Thus, for example, one book, which overlooked a fundamental distinction, was hailed by a reviewer as doing '. . . a clear and accurate hatchet job on the IQ test, which has been done before, but rarely to such good effect . . .'. When such judgements are expressed by those who are only spectators, misunderstanding is bound to be perpetuated and magnified.

Anyone who ventures onto the field of play must watch their front and rear. From the front will come the criticisms of the players who have first hand knowledge of the game. They will be only too aware of the simplifications, even over-simplifications, which have had to be made. They may be resentful that much of the jargon of their trade has been abandoned and many of the familiar landmarks removed. They may even question the motives for doing this. From the rear comes the plaintive cry of those who feel that anything as important as measuring intelligence should be expressible in terms that the layperson can understand, without summoning up more intellectual effort than required by a crossword puzzle. It is with the latter group in mind that the following reading strategy is suggested.

For most readers, it will not be sufficient simply to read the book, as one would a novel, from beginning to end. The following steps are suggested.

First skim through the whole book quickly. from start to finish. In this way you will become aware of the contents, the style of treatment and some of the principal conclusions.

Secondly, go through it more slowly but, when you meet what seem to be insuperable difficulties, leave them for later and press on so that the thread of the argument is not lost.

Focus, next, on the chapters which contain the key ideas leaving the others for later. It is at this stage that the serious work begins. Everyone should start with chapters 1 and 2 which provide much of the background and terminology. Skipping to chapter 13 will then enable you to preview the main conclusions, even though these may not be fully comprehensible at this stage. The heart of the book is in chapters 4, 5 and 6. These attempt to explain the basic underlying ideas on which an adequate understanding of the measurement problem rests.

They will need a good deal of attention and should be re-visited as your general understanding develops. Chapters 11 and 12 deal with two of the most highly controversial topics but are best left until last.

Finally, remember that many of the questions and criticisms which come to mind are probably dealt with somewhere even if they are not immediately recognisable.

Acknowledgements

This book is the result of many years of reflection and reading and it would be impossible now adequately to acknowledge, by name, all those who have contributed. Two of my colleagues at the London School of Economics, Martin Knott and Jane Galbraith, read early drafts of some of the chapters but their influence is more pervasive. Pat Lovie gave me the benefit of her detailed knowledge of the early history of intelligence testing by reading an early draft of chapter 2. My old friend, Karl Schuessler, offered wise advice as well as detailed comments at an early stage when my ideas were beginning to crystallise. Arthur Jensen responded speedily and courteously to my enquiries about his own work and provided much useful material. Several anonymous reviewers gave me the benefit of their more detached viewpoints. In reading these pages there may be others who will recognise unacknowledged influences from long ago. To all of these, I extend my warmest thanks.

As always, my greatest debt is to my wife, Marian, who can justly claim to have read almost every word. Having gone through the book-writing process together many times, it has become increasingly evident that two heads really are better than one.

1   The great intelligence debate: science or ideology?

The noise of battle

Almost everyone uses the word intelligence but it is one of those Humpty Dumpty words whose meaning is so elastic that it can cover virtually anything we choose. Lack of clarity does not make for rational discussion, but that simple fact is not enough to account for the ferocity with which the intelligence debate is often conducted. Every so often a spark ignites the dry tinder and the arguments flare up again. One of the most spectacular recent displays was triggered by the publication of *The Bell Curve* in 1994 by Herrnstein and Murray.[1] This book created quite a stir at the time and it has now become a point of reference for current exchanges – even if the temperatures are lower. It gave a new lease of life to a controversy with a long history going back at least to Sir Francis Galton towards the end of the nineteenth century.[2]

On the face of it, the book appeared to be a straightforward, thorough and clear exposition of a body of social science research. Its object was to explore how many of the problems affecting contemporary American society could be explained by variation in IQ (the intelligence quotient – a measure of intelligence) among individuals. It is clear from the flood of literature which followed in its wake, mainly highly critical, that there was much more to this than met the eye. The titles, alone, of some of the books which followed in response to *The Bell Curve* convey the strength of feeling which was engendered. *Measured Lies* was described on the cover as 'the most thorough and cogent analysis of the tangle of pseudo-science and moral dishonesty that comprises the frozen heart of *The Bell Curve*'. *Inequality by Design: Cracking the Bell Curve Myth* and *The Bell Curve Wars: Race, Intelligence and the Future of America* are two more examples of the same genre.[3] Writing in *Measured Lies*, Joyce King could hardly contain her contempt for the statistical treatment when she wrote 'The Bell Curve paradigm employs a number of "conjuring tricks", including statistical associations, that magically become causal relationships' (p. 182) and, again, 'I categorically reject the specious premise of the Bell Curve argument: that science has demonstrated that human intelligence, like height or weight, is a measurable, normally distributed natural law like thing in itself'(p. 185).

What *has* science demonstrated we may well ask? King's 'shot gun' approach could hardly fail to find a legitimate target somewhere. It is indeed true, as we shall see later, that the normality implied by the Bell Curve is a convention, not a fact, but the reason for this, and its implications, go much deeper than this superficial tirade comprehends. It is clear that *The Bell Curve* touched a raw nerve in some quarters and the reasons go very deep. Until we understand why this is so it will be impossible to get at the truth beneath the noise and fury.

It would be a mistake to jump to the conclusion that the storm occasioned by the publication of *The Bell Curve* was the product of the peculiar circumstances of America a decade or more ago and that it would blow itself out in due course. Surely, we might think, there are well tried methods by which such things can be investigated without the need for so much public excitement? One would have thought that the measurement of intelligence would have been one of those worthy but unexciting statistical activities – like the production of the Retail Prices Index – vital for the well-being of society but best left to those expert in these things. But this is not so, and the reason is that the whole question is bound up with our nature as persons. The 'hard' sciences like physics and chemistry seem to deal with hard facts about the physical nature of the world and scientists of all backgrounds can work together unencumbered by their ideological baggage. Everything changes as soon as we cross the frontier, and bring the human person into the picture. There is a deep cleavage in the approach to the scientific study of the human individual, not only between the scientific community and society at large but, more significantly, within the scientific community itself. In the 1960s the utterances of the Nobel prize-winning physicist William Shockley and the psychologist Arthur Jensen[4] touched a similarly raw nerve, to such an extent that the debate on intelligence ceased to be a purely intellectual contest and resulted in large-scale protests on American university campuses and, even, in some instances, in physical violence. The 'giant killer' on that occasion was Stephen Jay Gould whose book, *The Mismeasure of Man*, sought to demolish the arguments of the 'biological determinists' with a mixture of detailed examination of the evidence and verbal fisticuffs.[5] Gould returned to the fray with a new and enlarged edition in 1996 as his contribution to the debate on *The Bell Curve*. We shall return to this later, not only because it is one of the most cogent attacks, but because it seems to be widely regarded as the definitive refutation of the theoretical underpinnings of Herrnstein and Murray's case. Even Gould did not satisfy the likes of Joyce King because, to her way of thinking, his argument was conducted within a framework (paradigm was her term) which she saw as fundamentally flawed. Other, more modest but critical, treatments of the measurement of intelligence will be found in Richardson's *The Making of Intelligence* and Howe's *IQ in Question*. Among other contributions to the debate, less conspicuous perhaps, we shall take time to look at the arguments of Steven Rose in *Lifelines* where a number of widespread misapprehensions are given further currency.[6] Writers like these are sure to be quickly on the scene whenever the media decide to give the topic of intelligence a fresh airing.

Why such sensitivity?

It is worth spelling out, albeit in outline form, why intelligence is such a sensitive issue. Those on the right of the political spectrum tend to start with the primacy of the individual and the individual's freedom. Society, as they see it, is an aggregate of individuals and the ills of society are to be understood as arising from individual choices. Human diversity is to be encouraged. Equality is to be seen as equality of opportunity rather than of ability or achievement. Intelligence, like virtually all other human attributes, varies. A healthy and just society depends on recognising that fact and on the arrangement of its affairs so as to harness this diversity to serve the common good. Those on the left start at the other end, with society. It is society which moulds individuals as it constructs roles for them. The ability of individuals and the contributions they can make to society depend primarily on nurture. It is an egalitarian philosophy which sees inequality as arising from unjust social systems rather than from lack of enterprise or ability. When things go wrong the blame falls on society not the individual.

To some at least, the mere suggestion that people might vary in their innate abilities is deeply threatening. It places a fundamental inequality where ideology posits equality. Whereas inequalities created by an unequal distribution of resources can be remedied, any which are innate cannot be changed. They are made more pernicious by the alleged fact that these innate factors are perpetuated as they are passed down the generations in the genes. Money spent on schemes to eradicate innate inequality is thus money wasted trying to change the unchangeable.

In reality, this highly simplified caricature is complicated by a climate of mistrust, greed, the desire for power and all the other motives which commonly lie behind the propagation of high minded principles. Little wonder then that science is quickly branded as pseudo-science when it presumes to threaten such deeply held convictions.

The problem actually goes deeper still. It is not variation as such which causes the trouble. After all, we vary in our tastes in food and music. Some of us are tall and others short. Some are athletic and others are not. Except in rather restricted circumstances, such as among school children of a certain age, such things are not equated with feelings of inferiority or superiority. What is it about intelligence that links it so intimately with human worth?

It is obviously something to do with our brains, the seat of our consciousness, but it is what we do with those brains that counts. Intelligence is held to influence our ability to acquire power, influence and wealth. In short, those who have it in good measure are seen as being better endowed and able to lead a fuller life. Perhaps the link derives from the ultimate source of our values and beliefs; it may also have to do with the fact that they have changed in much of western society as a whole. The Judeo-Christian belief in 'Man made in the image of God' provided a sufficient basis for equality. With that fact securely in place, it was easy to be relaxed about other inequalities which spoke of the diversity of the creation rather than differences in worth. Without that foundation, one has to cast around for some other basis for ascribing worth to individuals. Science is seen, by some, as providing the only objective basis of knowledge and hence as the obvious route to a rational assessment of the human person. What is more natural then than to turn to a measure of our most distinctive and impressive attribute – our intelligence? For many therefore, intelligence and intelligence testing impinge on their understanding of themselves at the deepest level. It is hardly surprising that they find it hard to be rational about it.

What is intelligence?

We start with the term *intelligence* itself. It is clear from the way the word is used that we think of it partly, at least, as quantitative. People are described as being 'more' or 'less' intelligent. Dictionaries are the arbiters of what words are supposed to mean. In this case the *Shorter Oxford Dictionary* gives a wealth of material which focuses on the notion of 'understanding'. Thus it speaks of intelligence as: 'the faculty of understanding' and, more helpfully, as 'quickness of mental apprehension'. The quantifiability of intelligence, in common usage, is attested in 'understanding as a quality admitting of degree'. So far so good but none of this helps us very much in constructing a scale of measurement. Some would argue that, in spite of the way we use the word, intelligence cannot be measured at all. According to them the project falls at the first fence because it is futile to try to measure the immeasurable.

Before examining this argument it will help to look beyond the dictionary to see what the founding fathers of intelligence testing thought they were trying to measure. All of those quoted below were, or are, closely involved in the practice of measuring intelligence so let us see what they have to say.

Starting with David Wechsler who gave his name to widely used tests, it is:

. . . the aggregate or global capacity of the individual to act purposefully, to think rationally, and to deal effectively with his environment.

Sir Cyril Burt, one of the founding fathers of the intelligence testing movement, called it:

. . . innate general cognitive ability.

Even Howard Gardner, who some see as an opponent of IQ testing and as the originator of a richer and more relevant approach to human abilities says, of any 'intelligence':

To my mind, a human intellectual competence must entail a set of skills of problem solving – enabling the individual to resolve genuine problems or difficulties that he or she encounters and, when appropriate, to create an effective product – and must also entail the potential for finding or creating problems – and thereby laying the groundwork for the acquisition of new knowledge.[7]

Herrnstein and Murray opted for

. . . cognitive ability.

One definition, which it is claimed would cover what is contained in the *Handbook of Human Intelligence*,[8] is given by Sternberg and Salter in their introductory chapter as:

. . . goal-directed adaptive behaviour.

It seems clear enough that these various forms of words (and many others which could be quoted[9]) collectively justify the claim that we have a fairly clear idea, *in general terms*, of what we are talking about when we speak of 'intelligence'.

Unsympathetic writers have been more concerned to point to what they see as the triviality of some attempts at measuring intelligence by offering 'negative' definitions such as, for example, 'intelligence is not about doing tests'.[10] As a sign of desperation – or, maybe, terminal cynicism – some have turned the normal order of things on its head and defined intelligence, tongue in cheek perhaps, as 'what intelligence tests measure'.[11] The trouble, of course, is that there are many such tests and they do not necessarily all measure quite the same thing. An unambiguous definition in these terms would therefore have to pre-suppose universal agreement on the definitive test.

However, those seeking to ridicule the whole notion that intelligence can be measured at all (Michael Howe,[12] for example) merely see this negative approach as an 'own goal'. This definition appears to be no more than a tautology defining intelligence in terms of its own definition! This is a too superficial analysis and we shall have to return to the deeper issues after the foundations of our own argument are in place. For the moment it is sufficient to observe that the response depends entirely on the process by which the measure is constructed.

Even this brief excursion into the stormy waters of definition shows how easy it would be for the whole enterprise to be shipwrecked. For if we cannot define what it is that we wish to measure with precision, how can we expect to find an agreed measure? The more serious researchers have recognised this hazard and have sought an alternative route to the scientific study of mental abilities.

Charles Spearman[13] was, perhaps, the first a century ago, and he proposed to abandon the word altogether and substitute, in its place, the symbol g which referred to a quantity appearing in the new theoretical framework which he was proposing. Merely replacing a word by a symbol does not, of course, change anything and some would interpret it as no more than a smoke screen to confuse those who panic at the first sign of mathematics. However, that was not what Spearman actually did, as we shall see in chapter 2. He defined a process – or a model as we might call it today – which gave meaning to the concept. Arthur Jensen[14] followed Spearman in arguing that although the word 'intelligence' serves well enough in everyday language, it is too ambiguous for scientific use. He therefore called his major book on the subject *The g-Factor*.

There is a second quantity, usually abbreviated to IQ (for Intelligence Quotient), which figures more prominently than g in discussions of intelligence. It is often treated as if it were synonymous with 'intelligence' and, sometimes also, with g. These two quantities are central to the purpose of this book and, in separating the science from the ideology, it is crucial to understand that they are distinct entities. We shall return to this distinction shortly but, having made the point, there are some other issues to be dealt with first. The most important at this stage concerns whether intelligence can be measured at all. For if it cannot, there is little more to be said.

Can intelligence be measured?

Steven Rose[15] has long been adamantly opposed to what he calls the psychometric approach to intelligence testing and the subject re-surfaces in his book *Lifelines*. His treatment is based on misunderstandings which are quite common and therefore worth examining carefully.

Rose makes two basic criticisms. The first, which he calls *improper quantification*, is simply that things like intelligence cannot be quantified. The second, to which we shall come in a later chapter, relates to the use of the normal distribution in intelligence testing. The assumption, he writes, 'that any phenomenon can be measured and scored, reflects the belief . . . that to mathematize something is in some way to capture and control it' (p. 184). Thus, for example, the fact that some people are more violent than others does not, according to Rose, imply that the degree of violence which they display can be expressed on a numerical scale. This is even more true, he would argue, of intelligence. According to Rose, intelligence is a far more subtle and many-sided thing which makes it absurd to force it into the narrow mould of a single dimension. The alleged fallacy is that 'reified and agglomerated characters can be given numerical values'.

However, it is hard to make Rose's case without slipping into the very quantitative language which his argument sets out to undermine. A recent issue of the *Times Higher Educational Supplement*, for example, published an article by a philosopher (David Best) entitled 'Why I think intelligence cannot be tested.' Definitions of intelligence, the author writes, 'tend to be both tendentious and fallacious'.[16]

The problem is that the concept is twisted so that it can be empirically tested. According to the author, intelligence is not about doing tests, which tend to be concerned with speed of performance and such like, but about creativity and willingness to grapple with ideas. Not for the first time, we are reminded that Einstein was slow as a child and therefore, by contemporary testing standards, not very intelligent. Nevertheless, it emerged that the author thought that some sorts of intelligence could be measured and he, himself, spoke of 'lower intelligence' which surely implies that some people have less of it than others. Few, perhaps, would go as far as the newspaper columnist, quoted in note 10 of this chapter, who inverted the usual order of things by claiming that those who possessed what he regarded as true intelligence would find themselves at the bottom of the class if they deployed that attribute in IQ tests! The real burden of these complaints, as with so many other criticisms, is that intelligence is too subtle to admit of measurement on a simple linear scale.

This is true, and it is difficult to imagine that any serious investigator would wish to defend the proposition that all that is meant by the word intelligence can be captured by a single number. Indeed, that is one reason why most serious scholars, from Charles Spearman onwards, have been wary of using the term 'intelligence' at all. What is equally true is that we constantly make such comparisons by speaking and behaving as though some individuals were in fact more intelligent than others. How are we to reconcile these apparently conflicting views of the situation?

To anticipate a discussion, which can only be fully developed later, the answer lies in the fact that intelligent behaviour is not a one-dimensional phenomenon – it has many facets. We are very familiar with this sort of thing in other spheres and, in most contexts, it is entirely uncontroversial. Judges of ice skating know that the quality of performance cannot be adequately measured on a single dimension. So they rate skaters on two dimensions – artistic performance and technical merit. Wine tasters recognise several dimensions along which wines vary and any assessment of overall quality must somehow take all into account. Intelligence, as generally understood, is no different. There can therefore be no serious scientific claim to have captured this phenomenon in a single number. To assert otherwise is simply mischievous.

Thus far Rose, and those who think like him, are right, but it could turn out to be the case that there is one dominant dimension along which individuals vary much more than any other. Furthermore, if this same dimension were to emerge almost regardless of what set of test items were used, providing only that they reflected what we commonly understand by intelligent behaviour, then we might begin to suspect that it described something fundamental and important. What psychometricians, from Spearman onwards, have done is to focus on this particular major dimension, which seems to be important in describing human variability, and give it a name. The reason for calling it *g* was precisely to avoid the legitimate criticism that the term intelligence was not precise enough and not, as Rose fancifully speculates, to give it the fundamental status of the gravitational constant – also known as *g*![17] Rose is wrong to claim that 'reified and agglomerative characters' cannot be given numerical values. They obviously can and, as we shall see, factor analysis provides one way of doing this. What *can* and *must* be questioned is whether those numerical values adequately capture the essence of the comparison which we are making when we say, for example, that one person is more intelligent than another. This is an empirical question which has to be answered by bringing the data into dialogue with the usage of the term in everyday language.

Do measures of intelligence have any use?

However satisfied we might feel at having constructed a measure of intelligence, the exercise is pointless unless there is something useful which we can do with it. There are two ways of approaching this question. One is at the pragmatic level, where we ask whether it enables us to predict anything which it would be useful to know. For example, does it make selection for particular jobs more efficient? One of the early such uses was in the US air force where it was necessary to identify those with the ability to become good pilots. Educational selection was, perhaps, the major application envisaged. Binet's[18] motivation was to identify children who would benefit from extra help. Selection for different types of secondary education was the main use of intelligence tests in Britain after the Second World War. The fact that they are not now used on such a wide scale in education has more to do with changing ideas in education and society rather than the efficacy of the tests. In any case there is one important point to be made about the use of non-specific tests for general intelligence which is often overlooked. Selection for any particular task can probably be best made using a test designed specifically for that purpose. However, this may be a time-consuming and costly business. The value of a general test is that, although it will seldom be the best instrument available, it will serve a great variety of purposes adequately. It is useful to an employer in much the same way as is a university degree in literature or philosophy – it is an indication of general ability rather than a particular set of skills. As a general rule one might surmise that the less specific the test, the more widely useful it would be.

Testing has, traditionally, been seen as useful in the field of education, broadly interpreted. More recently its potential use in medicine has become apparent.

For example, mental tests can be used to monitor the progress of degenerative brain conditions such as Alzheimer's disease.

There is a second and less pragmatic kind of usefulness. If intelligence is an important human characteristic, it will have far-reaching implications for the way that society works and the life experience of its members. The just and efficient ordering of society depends, among other things, on being able to trace the lines of cause and effect linking policy decisions to outcomes. The authors of *The Bell Curve* were concerned to show that intelligence was a causal factor in a great many situations of social interest like poverty, income and marital stability. Whether or not individual differences are innate is clearly important if one wants to eliminate them. We are a long way from being able to say what is feasible or possible in some cases but these remarks show how much is at stake. The kind of question we should be asking is: does our measure explain anything in a coherent and clear fashion which, before it was available, was obscure? Is it an economical way of structuring our thinking in this particular field? Does it enable us to do anything useful that we could not do beforehand? Such questions lie behind the summing up in chapter 13.

Ideology re-visited

Now that we can view them in a broader context, it is helpful to return to the ideological questions raised earlier. The statistical exercise of constructing a measure of anything only becomes threatening at the point when it comes to be used. Measures of IQ were used by Herrnstein and Murray to investigate how far variables of social interest, like income or socioeconomic class, depend upon IQ. At first sight this may seem an innocent enough matter, but it is clear that many of the critics saw it as a thinly veiled attempt to advance a right wing political agenda. The authors of *The Bell Curve* were accused of pursuing a right-wing policy under the guise of social science. The alleged pernicious nature of the publication was magnified by the false picture which it presented to the world, at least as seen by many of its critics. A particularly critical matter concerned the hardly noticed transition from an empirical quantity like IQ to a more permanent characteristic of an individual envisaged as an unchanging, and perhaps unchangeable, personal attribute. Here we are back to fundamental questions about the nature of the human person and the threat posed by social science to deeply held views.

To illustrate how far beyond the boundaries of science the animosities run, it is instructive to trace the battle lines on the subject of funding. Opponents of *The Bell Curve* made much of the financial support provided by the Pioneer Fund. The fund was apparently founded in 1937 to promote the procreation of white families living in America before the Revolutionary War. According to Giroux and Searls, writing in *Measured Lies* (p. 79), this had been described by the London *Sunday Telegraph* as a 'neo-Nazi organisation closely integrated with the far right in American politics'. The message which comes across is that Herrnstein and Murray's work is a pseudo-scientific attempt to bolster up a pernicious doctrine and that the involvement of the Pioneer Fund is evidence of this. In short, tainted money cannot produce credible science.

The other side, unsurprisingly, saw things rather differently. Charles Murray in his Afterword to *The Bell Curve* pointed out that today's Pioneer Fund is very different from its origins. He claimed that of over a 1000 scholars whose work was cited in *The Bell Curve* his opponents could identify only thirteen who were funded by this 'tainted' source. In any case, most of these 'tainted' articles were published in reputable peer reviewed journals. From that side, the Fund was seen as having the courage to support fearless researchers who were prepared ask questions which the politically correct establishment would prefer to sweep under the carpet.

Neither side seemed over much concerned with whether the research was good science!

Our primary object in this book is to enable the reader to distinguish the science from the ideology. This is not to deny a place in policy making to extra-scientific matters. People have different beliefs and value systems and this fact is recognised in democratic societies where procedures exist to resolve the conflicts resulting from them. Scientific method, on the other hand, exists to discover those things about the world on which, given sufficient evidence, rational people should be able to agree. In matters of science we do not resort to the ballot box to resolve differences but to the data and the methods of analysing them. For this we need the expertise of those with the qualifications and experience to analyse the data. But who are the experts in this field?

Who are the experts?

To what kind of expert should we turn to resolve the often bitter disputes which rage in this field? Broadly speaking, the social sciences are concerned with the behaviour of people. Psychologists obviously have a strong claim to be heard as they study individual behaviour and have a long tradition of measuring aspects of it. Psychometricians, in particular, have made it their business to construct measures of all kinds of human ability. Historically, they were first on the scene with Charles Spearman's investigations of intelligence. We have noted that it was he who introduced *g* as the representation of what he believed to be the major dimension of human ability. His successors developed and elaborated his ideas, giving birth to factor analysis which has provided the theoretical framework for investigating these matters and to which we shall return. Sociologists have also staked their claim on the grounds that the development of human abilities takes place in the context of society and is strongly influenced by social interactions.

The claims to be heard do not stop there. Social scientists of all kinds have taken part in the debates and, given the extremely wide political implications of the conclusions, hardly anyone has felt excluded from taking part in the current arguments. Many of the contributors to the onslaught on Herrnstein and Murray were from university departments of education, cultural studies and suchlike.[19]

Economists have also been prominent in this field in the course of relating IQ to other social and economic variables where the analysis has been largely handled by econometric techniques.

Beyond the social sciences, geneticists can obviously claim a voice on account of the possible role of inheritance. Biology, also, has much to add about the environmental determinants of behaviour.

Public commentators, with no obvious scientific axe to grind, have also joined in the fray, bringing serious issues before a much wider public. The distinguished journalist Walter Lippmann, for example, in the 1920s, wrote a series of articles in *New Republic*. These were both well informed and highly critical of the US army tests of those times.

Underlying all these specialist interests is the methodology on which the construction of any measure depends. This, as we shall see, involves the collection and analysis of relevant data. Given the uncertainties of selecting both individuals and test items and the inherent variability of the material, this places the subject fairly in the territory of the statistician. It is, therefore, surprising that the professional experts in this field have, with very few exceptions, been conspicuously absent. The methodological weapons have largely been in the hands of those whose prime interest was in the subject matter. This has many advantages but, since new work on factor analysis, one of the key techniques, has taken a long time to percolate to the front lines of research, many contemporary treatments have a distinctly dated appearance. It is not unusual to find references being given to source books that are over a quarter of a century old.

Among those who have made a serious attempt to explain the methodology we may identify particularly Gould who has argued eloquently, if not always accurately, against the theoretical basis on which publications like *The Bell Curve* rests. Gould was a palaeontologist but best known as a popular science writer. He set out his statistical credentials in the second edition of *The Mismeasure of Man*. Since he is frequently quoted by lesser luminaries in the field as the one who has successfully demolished all the pretensions of the right-wing pseudo-scientists, we shall have to give special attention to his writings in chapter 7.

One secondary purpose of this book is to redress the disciplinary balance by bringing a statistician's voice into the debate. Fortunately, some have already been there but they have found it hard to make their voices heard above the clamour – much of it coming from the innumerate and ideologically motivated.

Scylla and Charybdis

The aim of this book is simple and needs to be clearly stated at the outset. It is about whether and how one can measure something like intelligence. This is not a simple matter. If it were, the endless disputes surrounding the subject would have been stifled at birth. It is not only a difficult matter but also an endlessly fascinating one. How can one capture and quantify something as elusive and yet as fundamental as intelligence? How, if at all, can it be brought within the purview of science.

Statisticians have long concentrated on how to extract the truth from numbers, but it has usually been assumed that the meaning of those numbers is unambiguous and straightforward. There is not much argument, for example, about what individual daily rainfall readings at a weather station actually mean. The interest lies in such things as how they vary over the seasons or from one day to the next. In many such fields it is typically assumed that we know how to measure the raw material and it is at that point that the real business starts. Here we are at a stage prior to that; before we can analyse measures of intelligence we must first know what intelligence means and be able to construct a measure in an acceptable way. To do this we shall have to provide a *framework* within which the main questions can be posed and answered. The term 'framework' conveys the key idea. It provides the language and the tools to make progress possible. In the case of intelligence, this framework is probabilistic and consists of a family of what are known as latent variable models. We shall explain what these terms mean later, but they have arisen to meet a widespread need in the social sciences at large. Intelligence is not an isolated case. There are many other measurement problems in social science which share the same characteristics. Most of them lack the ideological overtones of intelligence and hence have gone largely unnoticed.

There have been several attempts in recent years to bring the intelligence debate back to the facts of the case. A necessary starting point for approaching any controversial subject is to get the facts of the matter straight. Since it is commonly claimed that those purporting to convey facts have biased or distorted the truth, one cannot be too careful about one's sources. In the wake of the publication of *The Bell Curve*, the American Psychological Association sought to separate the science from the ideology by appointing a task force. The membership was chosen to cover a wide range and their report, which was published in 1996, can be consulted in Neisser, 1996. Another excellent starting point is *Intelligence: A Very Short Introduction* by Ian Deary (Deary 1996). Although it is brief, this book aims to take the reader to the actual sources on which the accumulated knowledge depends. The author, in his introduction, says '. . . it is facts that drive the present book. It is an attempt to cut out the middle man and put you in touch with some actual research data in human intelligence.'

Behind the data, of course, lie the test items. They are the questions, problems and puzzles which subjects are required to tackle. There appears to be a ready market for books of the *Test Your Own IQ* variety and, in addition, tests can now be found on the Web. Constructing test items is a serious matter but, although pursuing the topic here might prove to be an entertaining diversion, it would contribute nothing to the main thrust of this book.[20]

We shall not seek to duplicate any of these of contributions because this book is not, primarily, about the data; it is about what can be legitimately learned from the data.

Just as we do not intend to repeat what is already well documented on the empirical side, so we do not intend to claim that all outstanding questions can be given definitive answers. While uncertainty is seen as a weakness among politicians and others who have causes to advocate, it is a strength in science. Knowledge in science is always partial and acknowledgement of that fact needs no apology. We shall, therefore, be as much concerned with what cannot be known as with what can. To be scientific we need to be able to quantify intelligence, for numbers are the raw material of science. Science is about generalisation and illumination is to be had by seeing things in a wider context. This leads to a sense of proportion in every sense of the word.

The most challenging aspect of the whole enterprise is to elucidate this framework without using mathematics. This is daunting because mathematics is the natural language of quantity. Without it, the clarity for which we strive is almost unattainable. With it, the goal is almost entirely obscured for those for whom mathematics is a foreign language. Perhaps the most apt word is 'accessible'. The aim is to provide access to those who have both the interest and the need to judge these thorny issues for themselves. We aim to steer a middle course between the Scylla of over-simplified popularity and the Charybdis of accurate but highly technical treatment.

2   Origins

The two roots

The seeds of a potential source of confusion have already been sown by the use of several different terms. We started by talking about intelligence, then we slipped into referring to IQ and had to note that it was a measure of intelligence. Finally we mentioned something called g, or the g-factor, and used it much as though it were just another name for intelligence. These terms are, most emphatically, not synonyms. They are often treated as if they were and therein lies much of the confused thinking which muddies the waters of current debates. The roots of this muddle lie, to a large extent, in the vagaries of history, and it is to history, therefore, that we turn to begin to unravel the tangled threads.

Two routes may be traced from the origins of intelligence testing to the present day and it is interesting that there appears to have been little constructive interaction between them in the early stages. The first, which gave rise to the term IQ, started with Alfred Binet around 1905 and reached its zenith with the appearance of Lewis Terman's, *The Measurement of Intelligence* published in 1916. The second strand has its roots in Charles Spearman's pioneering paper of 1904 on factor analysis.[1] Binet reviewed Spearman's paper unfavourably in the following year and Spearman, for his part, was no more impressed with Binet's work. Terman referred briefly to Spearman's contribution, among others, but in a manner which suggested that it added little to his own work. A link between the two branches seems to have arisen out of the need to extend Binet's method for children to adults in the 1930s. This was done by David Wechsler, who had studied briefly with Spearman.[2]

In order to understand the contemporary scene it is therefore important to know something about factor analysis, because this is the main technique underlying the measurement of intelligence. First, however, we shall look at the origins of the Intelligence Quotient, or IQ.

Origins of IQ: Binet, Terman and Wechsler

In the extensive literature of the debate about IQ there is rarely any recognition of the fact that the term is hardly ever used today in its original sense. Gould and others fail to note that it all began with the attempt by Binet to measure the intelligence of children. He, and those who followed him, were interested in the educational process and wanted some measure which would tell them how advanced or retarded a given child was. The fact that their discussion was set in a different age, when it was permissible to talk about eugenics and 'feeblemindedness', seems to have diverted attention away from the technical aspects of what the pioneers were trying to do.

Binet's original idea was refined by others and is, perhaps, most clearly expounded in Terman's book. The key idea behind IQ, as originally defined, was that the level of performance of a child in a test could be expressed by reference to the age at which the average child would be able to achieve that level of performance. Thus arose the concept of *mental age* (MA). To have a mental age of seven meant that the child performed like the typical ('average') seven-year-old. By comparing the mental age with the chronological age it was then possible to say whether the child was advanced or retarded and by how much.

The mental age was calculated as follows. Suppose we give a battery of test items to nine-year-old children, say, and calculate their average score. This average is interpreted as defining the point on the scale at which the typical nine-year-old is located. Any child of whatever age who attains this score is said to have a mental age of nine. In the same way we can establish typical scores for children of all ages. The mental age of any particular child is then found by seeing where their individual score lies in relation to these benchmark scores.

The question then arose as to how best to measure the difference between the two. One obvious possibility was to take the simple difference and say, for example, that the child was two years ahead or behind the typical child of the same age. The trouble with this measure was that it changed as the child grew older; for example, a four-year-old who was one year ahead would, it was found, be rather more than one year ahead by the time he reached the age of seven. If we are aiming to measure some constant ('innate') characteristic of the individual, which we do not expect to change much with age, we need to look for some measure of the difference between mental and chronological age which does not depend on (is 'invariant' with) age. The choice of the early investigators, following Wilhelm Stern[3] in 1912, was to divide the mental age by the chronological age. The result of dividing one quantity by another is called the *quotient*. Hence it was appropriate to call the result of dividing the mental age (MA) by the chronological age (CA) the *Intelligence Quotient* (IQ). For practical convenience, following Terman, the result of the above calculation has traditionally been multiplied by 100. Thus, for example, if a child of five years (CA) performs like the typical child of six years (MA) then their IQ is $(6/5) \times 100 = 120$. When that child reaches the age of ten one would then expect their IQ to be the same, which would imply their mental age to be 12 (=120 × 10/100).

The foregoing description leaves a great deal unsaid. How the test is constructed and what kind of test items are used is, of course, absolutely crucial. In order to justify calling IQ a measure of intelligence, the test items have to be defensible as indicators of intelligent behaviour. Questions of this kind are the main preoccupation of Terman's book. We shall have to return to this issue in chapter 3, when we consider how Binet's original approach relates to the factor analysis approach which has dominated recent debates. The central claim that IQ originally related the mental age to the chronological age of children makes the essential point for the moment.

As noted above, IQ, as originally defined, was designed for use with children. It was clearly unsatisfactory for adults because, although mental ability obviously increases during the years of childhood, it levels off somewhere between the ages of fourteen and eighteen. It does not, therefore, remain fixed through life. If one were to calculate IQ in the above manner, a point would be reached when mental age would cease to increase while chronological age continued on its upward path. The effects of this would be to make IQ begin to decrease around the mid teens This problem could be dealt with by treating chronological age as if it were fixed from the age of fifteen or sixteen onwards. Thus, for adults, the divisor in the IQ equation would be held constant and so an adult's IQ would be, essentially, proportional to their mental age.

However, it subsequently turned out that IQ, measured in this way, was not a precisely fixed quantity throughout childhood either – at least at the extremes of the ability range. In the course of time, intelligence tests were increasingly needed for adults, especially young adults. It was clear that the original definition had to be reconsidered and this led to the old definition being replaced by a new one proposed by David Wechsler[4] around 1939. The Wechsler definition requires us to divide the individual's total score by the average score obtained by people of the same age. This is still a quotient and the result can be properly described as the Intelligence Quotient but it must be emphasised that it is not quite the same as the original IQ. This measure does seem to be more nearly constant through life, other things being equal, and can therefore be used over the whole life span.

The new measure met with some criticism because there seemed to be no natural unit of measurement in which it could be expressed. Mental and chronological ages, on the other hand, were expressed in the familiar units of age and the IQ resulting from them had a meaning which was easy to grasp.

Wechsler recognised the problem and concluded that there was no natural unit in which IQ could be measured. Nor was it easy to define a zero point for the scale. It is true that an individual with no ability would obtain the lowest possible score (zero if all scores were non-negative) but this would be far away from the bulk of the sample. In coming to the conclusion that the origin, scale and, in fact, the distribution of IQ scores was arbitrary, Wechsler showed great insight. Nevertheless, he still had the problem of choosing a common scaling which would enable IQs from different times and places to be compared. He did this by bringing his scale into line with that which had become familiar from the Terman IQ. Those considered to have 'normal' intelligence had been assigned scores in the interval 90–110. These limits contain half the population. Wechsler therefore scaled his IQs so that they had an average of 100, and so that the same proportion was contained within these limits. In modern parlance, he scaled his measure so that it had an average of 100 and a standard deviation of fifteen.

Wechsler, therefore, had produced a new way of constructing an IQ index which could be used at all ages and which was measured on a familiar scale. It appears to have quickly superseded the old measure and is still in use today.

The existence of two IQs might have been expected to give rise to confusion and controversy but this seems to have been minimal and there is a good reason for this. To see why, we might ask: 'Under what conditions would the two measures give the same value?' The answer turns out to be: 'If the average score at any age is proportional to age.'[5] This is clearly not the case over the whole age range, but it is approximately true over short intervals, such as the childhood years. In effect, therefore, the 'new' IQ was approximately the same as the old over the range for which the latter was designed, but had the advantage of being valid for the whole age range.

Wechsler did not pay great attention to the form of the frequency distribution which should be adopted for IQ. He chose the normal distribution (the so-called 'Bell Curve') largely, one assumes, because the old IQ had had a distribution which was roughly normal. What is quite clear, however, is that he knew that any choice was quite arbitrary and all that his process of measurement justified was a ranking of individuals. In this he was far ahead of his time. It is particularly important to remember this because the 'Bell Curve' seems to have entered the public consciousness as part of the essence of IQ. It is ironic that something so insubstantial should have been chosen as the title of one of the most controversial books of our time.

From Wechsler's definition it is a small step to dropping the denominator altogether. For adults, their average score at any age would be roughly the same and so IQ is, for practical purposes, equivalent to the individual's score. The standardised score could therefore be used as a measure in its own right. This consideration, in fact, brings us to the point of convergence of the Binet branch and that originating from Spearman. It does, however, sometimes lead to confusing statements such as 'IQ increases up to the mid-teen years.' This is directly contrary to what the original IQ was supposed to measure – namely something which did not change with age! In its original sense, it was designed specifically *not* to increase. What actually increases is the test score and this is only a substitute for IQ for *adults*. This sort of confusion has been carried over into general thinking about intelligence and is still responsible for much muddled thinking today.

Viewed in this way, IQ has much in common with other indices familiar in everyday life. Share price indices, for example, track the general level at which shares are traded. Some shares rise and others fall but what the market wants is some general indication of the direction in which things are moving. Just as IQ is a kind of average of many test scores, so a share index is an average of many share prices. Price indices charting the 'cost of living' are other examples of the usefulness of indices which summarise a multitude of indicators.

In view of claims we shall make later, it will be as well to make one or two things clear at this stage. There is nothing in the definition of an index of intelligence which says what causes the variation in IQ. It could be inherited or it could be environmental or some mixture of the two. One further point we have already made also bears repeating. The choice of items to include in a test is more important than how the scores are combined. It is the set of items which reveals what it is we think we are measuring. IQ can be thought of as a collective property of that set.

Another crucial point, which will be underlined repeatedly, is that these measures of IQ, like others to which we shall come, are population dependent. That is an IQ of 100 is not an absolute measurement of anything. It is simply the score assigned to someone whose ability lies at the centre of the distribution for the population under study. If it were possible to devise an appropriate IQ test for the inhabitants of some remote planet of super-intelligent individuals, their superiority would not show in their IQ scores. All that these would tell us is where any individual lay in relation to other members on that planet. Inter-planetary differences could not be detected because our method of standardising the scores starts off by giving each planet the same average score.

Origins: Charles Spearman and factor analysis

This strand of development might be traced back to Sir Francis Galton[6] whose *Hereditary Genius* attempted a study of how human ability was handed down through the generations. This, combined with the early work of Karl Pearson on correlation, laid the foundations for the scientific study of human attributes and their inheritance. But the real credit must go to Charles Spearman who invented factor analysis which, in its modern guise, provides the theoretical underpinning for the measurement of intelligence.

Factor analysis, itself, has been the subject of much learned dispute among the experts. Wider debate has often been at second hand because of the difficulty which many have of penetrating the highly technical character of the literature on the subject. Even so popular an expositor as Gould confessed to difficulty in finding an appropriate way of getting the essentials across.[7] His solution to the problem is contained in *The Mismeasure of Man* where he relies largely on pictorial methods. Unfortunately, his account is not entirely accurate and, since it has been so widely regarded as definitive, we shall provide a critique in chapter 7. Factor analysis proved to provide a much richer framework in which to develop a theory of measurement and it lies at the heart of this book. In order to set the scene and to provide a historical perspective for the more technical aspects, we shall briefly trace the path by which this point was reached.

Factor analysis, as we have said, was invented by Charles Spearman and it first appeared in a paper which he wrote in 1904 entitled '"General intelligence" objectively determined and measured'. It was a remarkable achievement. At a time when theoretical statistics was in its infancy and multivariate analysis, as we now know it, was half a century in the future, Spearman provided a technique which has been behind a vast amount of subsequent applied psychological research. Spearman's original aim was to provide a more objective means of judging the abilities of school children. It was generally accepted that children varied in ability and that their teachers were in the habit of grading them on the basis of subjective judgements. Spearman was interested in the question of whether more objective measures, such as response times, could be used to put the measurement on a more secure basis. The first part of that exercise involved constructing some kind of scale of measurement for subjective assessments which were based on many indicators. The idea behind this was a very simple one depending on the idea of the degree of correlation between two variables. At first sight this seems to have nothing in common with Binet's idea but, as so often happens in scientific work, initial appearances are deceptive.

Spurious correlation

The strength of the relationship between two sets of scores is usually measured by their correlation coefficient. If a high score on one quantity tends to be associated with a high score on the other, then the correlation will be positive and somewhere in the range 0,1; the larger the value, the stronger the correlation. A correlation of 0 means that there is no interdependency between the two variables at all; a correlation of 1, that there is an exact (linear) relationship. Saying that variables are linearly related is equivalent to saying that the same kind of relationship exists between them as exists between temperatures expressed on the Celsius and Fahrenheit scales of temperature. The numbers are different but if we plot them, the points lie on a straight line. A set of temperatures expressed on the two scales will thus be perfectly correlated. Given the temperature on one scale, we can always read off that on the other from the straight-line relationship.[8]

The central idea behind factor analysis is closely related to what is often known as *spurious correlation*. Elementary courses in statistics have been enlivened for generations by amusing examples of this phenomenon. Every student learns, though many subsequently forget, that correlation does not imply causation. That is, just because two variables happen to be correlated, one is not justified in inferring that either is the cause of the other. One such example is the purported correlation between the size of feet and quality of handwriting in children. Suppose that it is, indeed, true that children with larger feet also score more highly in handwriting tests. No one would seriously argue that there is some causal link between the size of feet and how well the child can write. One can, however, easily understand why this correlation might come about. Both handwriting and foot size depend upon age and the older the child the larger will be their feet, in general; also, the older the child the better their handwriting is likely to be (up to a certain age, at any rate!). The observed correlation is therefore described as spurious because it does not imply any causal link between the two variables. It arises because both have a common causal factor in the shape of the child's age.

When such correlations occur in practice, it may not be immediately obvious whether or not there is a common cause operating on both variables and, if so, what it is. Nevertheless, we may always speculate that there is some such common cause, even if we cannot immediately identify it. Suppose, instead of having two variables like foot size and handwriting ability, we have a whole collection, all of which are mutually correlated. We may again speculate that this correlation arises from some common factor operating at a deeper level. This is the case when children take a number of tests in arithmetic, say, which we believe all depend upon a basic set of skills and which it is the object of the test to uncover. The scores on the individual items are certainly indicative of the child's ability but we feel that, lying behind them, there is something more fundamental which we may describe as arithmetical ability. This is not peculiar to one particular set of test items but would exert its influence on the results of any other set of similar arithmetical test items.

If, therefore, it turned out that scores on all pairs of a set of tests were positively correlated, that fact would be indicative of a possible common underlying cause of the correlation. The problem then is to identify what that source is and to find some means of extracting from the tests whatever information there is about this common source.

Spearman's basic idea

The basic idea behind factor analysis is based on the following simple proposition which follows from what we have just said about the reasons for spurious correlation. If the set of test items which we observe depends upon a common ability, then we would expect those who have higher levels of ability to tend to do better on all tests. This would give rise to the positive correlations just referred to. A crude approach to constructing a measure of that ability would be simply to add up the scores on all the items; the good students would tend to have high marks on all tests and so obtain a high total. This, after all, is what teachers have been doing for generations when they add up marks given to individual questions on an examination paper or when they add up test scores obtained over a period of time.

What is wrong, we may ask, with this simple expedient which has served so well for so long? What factor analysis aims to do is to provide a framework for deciding whether adding up in this fashion really is the best way of extracting the relevant information and, if not, to suggest something better.

This proposition contains the source of one of the main problems of interpretation which we meet when using factor analysis as a technique for measuring intelligence. It is certainly true that, if individuals vary in a particular kind of ability, then those with higher ability will tend to do better on the test items. The converse, however, is not necessarily true. It does not follow that if a set of test scores is correlated that their correlation must have arisen from their common dependence upon some underlying variable, like intelligence. One possible alternative explanation arises when the sequence of test scores are ordered in time. There may then be serial dependence between successive scores in the sequence. Each element is therefore dependent upon the one which precedes it and not on any underlying variable. Such a process may lead to a set of positively correlated variables which might mislead us into supposing that the correlations are indicative of the presence of some common influence.

Spearman's two-factor theory

Returning to our main theme, Spearman proposed what came to be known as his *two-factor theory*. He supposed that the score on any test item was composed of two parts. The first part was supposed to reflect the common ability required by all the tests and the second part what was specific to each particular item. Hence the term *two-factor*; one part being called the *common factor*, the other part the *specific factor*. It is the common factor in which we are primarily interested and the aim of Spearman's analysis was to separate out the common element from the specific factors. Behind this simple idea we can already see the rationale for adding up test scores to give an indication of the underlying variable. Thus one might suppose that the specific factors would be independent of the common factor and hence that they would sometimes push the observed score in one direction and sometimes in the other in a symmetrical fashion. The net effect when averaged over a fairly large number of items might then be to produce a cancelling out of the effects of the specific factors. In chapter 7 we shall develop this idea to give a basic understanding of what factor analysis is and what it aims to do. For the moment we take it as given that ways can be found of separating the common and the specific factors.

Burt, Thurstone and Thomson

Spearman was not the only person interested in factor analysis. Others joined him and, over a period of forty years, he continued to develop and apply the two-factor model. Chief among his co-workers, and Spearman's successor at University College London, was Sir Cyril Burt. Burt is now remembered (unjustly, perhaps) for allegations of having falsified data and for having invented fictitious collaborators in order to bolster his belief in the heritability of intelligence.[9] These matters are still in dispute but are not central to our present concerns. He may be justly viewed as the first person to apply Spearman's methods, in a major paper in 1909. In this work he put the two-factor theory on a firmer empirical foundation than had Spearman himself. Later, as adviser to the London County Council, Burt had access to very large amounts of data relating to the testing of school children and he thus became a pioneer in the application of factor analysis. Spearman's hand is evident in the theoretical parts of Burt's paper, and in later years, Burt appears to have somewhat exaggerated his own theoretical contributions.[10]

It was not long before other, independent, researchers began to discover the limitations of the Spearman method. Sets of test scores were obtained which could not be adequately explained by the two-factor hypothesis.

Something more seemed to be needed to account for the patterns of their correlations. Much, of course, depended upon how the test items were chosen, but it soon became apparent that the data could often be more plausibly explained on the supposition that more than one type of ability was involved. One might have guessed, for example, that verbal and spatial abilities were distinct and that the correlations within those groupings might be higher than between them. This, indeed, turned out to be the case. Thorndike, who published a book on the measurement of intelligence in 1927, was an early critic who engaged in debate with Spearman. However, the major methodological advance came from Thurstone who, from the early 1930s, developed his multiple factor hypothesis which became the main competing theory to that of Spearman.[11] Thurstone claimed that there was a cluster of distinct abilities which contributed to the performance of individuals in tests. He extended Spearman's two-factor model to a multiple factor model which became the basis of much subsequent factor analysis. Spearman clung tenaciously to his two-factor model to the end of his life though he did come to recognise, rather grudgingly, that other factors, besides his general factor, g, might have parts to play. These secondary factors became known as group factors because they were held to influence only a limited number of the test items. In fact, as we shall see, the gap between Spearman and Thurstone was not as large as the two main protagonists and their supporters supposed. Indeed, the source of the confusion between them proves to be one of the most fundamental matters in understanding contemporaries disputes.

Godfrey Thomson was an educational psychologist working, first at Armstrong College, Newcastle and then at the University of Edinburgh.[12] He, too, saw the weaknesses of Spearman's approach and proceeded to demonstrate that a set of positive correlations did not necessarily imply the two-factor model which Spearman had proposed. His idea has been taken up by others and has also been used recently by Mackintosh 1998 (p. 226), to show that g is not the only possible explanation for positive correlations. Thomson supposed that responding to a test item made use of a sample of a number of elementary processes. If two items both made use of a large proportion of these processes, the likelihood is that they would have a large proportion of them in common and this, the theory supposed, would lead to a high correlation between the scores. The converse would be true if few processes were called into play but, always, the correlation would be positive. The positive correlations, therefore, would arise from the utilisation of common processes and not from varying ability. Demonstrating that what is observed empirically admits of more than one explanation both curbs over-confidence in one's theories and provides a powerful stimulus for further investigation. However, as we shall note later, Thomson's idea does not account so readily for the pattern of differences in the correlations as does the 'underlying' variable idea.

We have already noted the lack of interaction between the 'IQ' and 'g' schools of thought and such evidence as there is suggests that much of their work proceeded in a state of mutual ignorance. Herbert Henry Goddard was one of those in the IQ camp who thought that data gained from practical applications were far more valuable than abstract theoretical arguments. Nevertheless, Leila Zenderland reports that Goddard did take notice when Cyril Burt included some of Spearman's ideas in his studies of children. She quotes Goddard as saying, 'At least it is comforting to find that the existence of a general intelligence has already been arrived at by an entirely different method of approach.'[13]

Hierarchical factor analysis

An apparent resolution of the conflict between Spearman and Thurstone was provided by what came to be called hierarchical factor analysis. This was done by treating the factors in exactly the same way as the original indicators. After all, if one can interpret the positive correlation between indicators as evidence for a common underlying factor, then one can treat a set of correlated factors in precisely the same way. Thus, if human performance on a varied set of test items could be described by a cluster of correlated abilities, then there is no reason why one should not analyse the correlations between those abilities in the same manner as the original variables. If one arrived at, say, five such abilities from the primary factor analysis which were positively correlated among themselves, that fact could be regarded as indicative of some common source on which they all depended; that is, a more fundamental underlying variable at a deeper level. That, indeed, turned out to be the case and so Spearman's g duly re-emerged as the ultimate explanation of the original correlations. It was thus possible for the multiple-factor model of Thurstone and the two-factor model of Spearman to co-exist. One could allow that there were indeed multiple or group factors while continuing to maintain that underlying them all was a single basic dimension of ability which Spearman had named g. In later chapters we shall argue that this is not necessarily the most fruitful way to resolve the alternative accounts given by the two approaches, but it does serve to underline the degree of arbitrariness which is present in the interpretation of all factor models.

Early limitations of factor analysis

Spearman's factor analysis was a technique which was born before its time. In modern parlance, it is a highly computer intensive procedure for which adequate computing facilities were lacking for half a century until after the end of the Second World War. Much of the early literature is taken up with the illustration of short cuts of one kind or another designed to make the arithmetic easier. This concentration on arithmetical problems tended to obscure many more funda-mental issues which have only come to the fore since the computing aspects were rendered trivial by modern computers. The devices to which practition-ers had to resort smacked of the doings of a secret society which attracted the suspicions of those who had not been initiated into the art. Although many of those involved in the early development of factor analysis had a mathematical background, the impact of statisticians was not great; many who, otherwise, might have contributed to the development of the subject, were often scornful of what they regarded as arcane mysteries. The result was that the subject was distorted by the exigencies of practical needs and computational difficulties.

Latterly, factor analysis has become enormously popular and its use has extended far beyond its original object of constructing measures of human abilities. Indeed, its use has often been pushed far beyond the limits of what can be justified, but that is a story for another occasion.

Modern factor analysis

The Second World War marks a watershed in the history of factor analysis. The change was signalled not only by the advent of the electronic computer, which did not have its full impact until the coming of desktop computers in the 1980s, but more significantly by the transition from being a technique practised by psychologists to its present place in the statisticians' armoury. This was facilitated by the influential book *Factor Analysis as a Statistical Method* by Lawley and Maxwell, first published in 1963.[14] Equally significant, but not obvious at the time, was the introduction of latent structure analysis by Paul Lazarsfeld. He recognised that there was a connection between the earlier factor analysis and the new methods which he was introducing into sociology.[15] However, by emphasising the differences rather than the similarities, he diverted attention from the common structure which they share. The only essential difference between factor analysis and latent structure analysis is in the type of variable with which each deals. In factor analysis, all the variables, observable and unobservable, are continuous, that is they are things like length or money where any value in some range is possible. In latent structure analysis, on the other hand, some of the variables are categorical which means that they can only be identified by which of several categories they fall into. The simplest categorical variables have only two possible categories like yes/no or right/wrong. Seen with the benefit of hindsight, Lazarsfeld's failure to grasp this point fully was, perhaps, one of the greatest obstacles to the development of latent variable modelling on modern lines.

With the coming of powerful desktop computers there was the incentive to develop software packages which could implement the methods of factor analysis and, after a hesitant start, efficient programs are now readily available in the major commercial software packages.

Over the past two decades there has been a slow but definite trend towards full integration of factor analysis into the mainstream of modern statistical practice with great benefits to all parties. This goes far beyond the purely technical aspects of what is still a highly sophisticated technique but gives greater insight into the meaning of what a factor is and hence into what kind of a thing is the quantity known as g.

Learning from history

This digression into the history of the subject identifies the two main roots from which the present position has developed. From it we may extract four themes which will figure prominently in what follows.

First, that the variation in test scores among individuals can often be successfully explained in terms of latent variation among individuals at a deeper level.

Secondly, that this latent variation often needs more than one dimension to describe it adequately. This raises the question of how to interpret multidimensional variation and whether any further summarisation is possible or useful.

Thirdly, that measurements of intelligence are relative to a particular population. They cannot be used for comparisons between populations without making further assumptions.

Fourthly, our review draws attention to a fundamental question which we have not so far properly addressed, though it was briefly mentioned earlier. This, in the terminology of factor analysis, is known as the problem of *factor scores*. That is, how do we locate individuals on the ability scale thus arriving at a number (or numbers) which purports to reflect their ability? Or, in simpler language: how do we turn the individual's test scores into a measure of their intelligence? In the Binet approach the IQ index did this in such a direct way that the question scarcely arose. In factor analysis it is not quite so obvious how this should be done. This, of course, is one of the main problems which underlies the present project, namely, how do we measure g?

3 The end of IQ?

The parting of the ways

We have outlined two approaches to measuring intelligence. The IQ route involves, essentially, computing an average test score in much the same way as we construct other indices. The other approach, using factor analysis, remains something of a mystery at this stage whose depths remain to be explored. It is now time to stand back and view the problem of measuring intelligence from first principles and then to form a judgement on the best way forward. Our conclusion will be that the emphasis on IQ in the past has been misplaced and that, in an ideal world, it would be abandoned. However, there seems little chance of that happening. So it is worth seeing whether a reasonable justification for its use can be given and whether the objections raised against it are well founded. This will also pave the way for the introduction of its main competitor, g. Our strategy in this chapter is, therefore, to expose the weaknesses of the 'index' approach by making the best case for it that we can!

Such an evaluation certainly cannot be made effectively from a purely historical perspective, because the concepts on which the measurement of intelligence depends have only emerged slowly over a century. Indeed, much of the current confusion arises from a lack of clarity about the conceptual framework – often because the protagonists have adopted the outlook of the pioneers and failed to take new work on board. Intelligence is not unique in this respect.[1] There are many other quantities measured by indices, like quality of life, cost of living and conservatism, which present similar problems. The main difference is that the latter do not carry the same ideological overtones.

Intelligence is not so much a 'thing' as a collective property

The first thing to get clear is that intelligence, however we measure it, is a summarising concept which has been created for use in human discourse. There are a great many things which people do and say which seem to depend on a common kind of basic mental ability. When we say that James is more intelligent than Jeremy, we expect our hearers to know what we mean. If challenged to defend the statement, we would probably begin to list tasks which James performs more successfully than Jeremy. This list might be long or short depending on how well we know the individuals concerned and how well considered our judgement is. Some one else might come to the same or a different judgement according to the meaning they attach to the word 'intelligence' or to the particular indicators they use to form their judgement. Such variation is normal in everyday matters and, though it might justly give rise to argument, seldom causes too much trouble.

The attempt to *measure* intelligence on a numerical scale calls for something more precise. It requires a greater depth of understanding of what we actually mean by the term. We suggest below how such a degree of precision may be approached but first we repeat that, whatever else it is, intelligence is a *collective property*. We used the word 'indicator' above to mean a test item which reveals something about the degree of intelligence possessed by the individual on whom it is observed. This may be the successful performance of a task or something more informal like a particularly perceptive remark. Whatever it is, we feel we have learnt something from it about the intelligence of the subject. Furthermore, the more indicators we have, the more confident we are likely to feel about our assessment. What we understand 'intelligence' to mean, therefore, is expressed, however imperfectly, by the collection of test items we choose. This is what we mean by saying that intelligence is a collective property. The problem is to capture it.

Collective properties are familiar to us all and we could hardly manage without them. Politicians are very prone to claim to know what 'the people of this country think, or want'. 'The people' in this context is a collective entity to which views are imputed almost as if it was a single person. In one sense this is a fiction, but it is a very useful fiction and no politician would take kindly to the suggestion that 'the people' did not exist or was not real.

To take what is, perhaps, the best-known example, consider the humble average. Everyone knows what an average is. If we have the weekly expenditure of 10,000 families in a town, we may summarise the expenditures by finding the average. This is a single figure which tells us something useful about how much families, as a whole, in that town spend. It certainly does not tell us everything but it would be useful for comparing the levels of expenditure in different towns, for example. The average is a collective property of the 10,000 individual expenditures. It captures the general level of expenditure and we use such figures all the time without ever questioning their meaning. All but the least sophisticated recognise that there is an important difference between a collective measure, such as an average, and a single measure of income. The average does not apply to any particular individual. Comedians have long managed to squeeze a mite of laughter out of the statement that the average family consists of, say, 1.6 children but the apparent incongruity of that statement illustrates our point. Collective properties are quite distinct from individual properties even though they are derived from them.

Similar, but slightly more sophisticated, examples of such collective properties are provided by share-price indices and measures of the cost of living. A share-price index is a collective property of the set of prices, many thousands perhaps, at a particular time. It encapsulates an important property of a large number of indicators (individual prices) in a single number which forms part of the decision making of many individuals and institutions. Indeed, it sometimes seems to take on an existence of its own as when commentators speak of an index as 'breaking the psychologically important 4000 barrier'. In reality, the 4000 point on the scale has no significance of itself. The fact that it is a round number is merely a consequence of our having chosen to count in tens and has nothing to do with economic realities. Nevertheless, people confer a reality on the number which makes it have real effects in the world. In much the same way, intelligence is an index of an individual's performance of a set of tasks.

A further, more subtle, example is provided by 'personality' which we refer to as though it were a 'thing' but it is actually a complex summary of many attributes – in other words, a collective property.

A collective property of what?

There is a long tradition of constructing economic and social indices and the Terman tradition[2] in psychology may be viewed as an extension of those ideas to the realm of intelligence testing. Share-price indices, retail-price indices, indices of industrial production and suchlike are all averages of some kind and few are disposed to dispute that they measure what they are claimed to measure. This is not usually from close personal knowledge but from a willingness to trust the experts. Why, then, is there so much argument when these widely accepted procedures are extended into the intelligence field? Are there no experts there who can be trusted to do the job? This is doubtless what many feel but there is also a more fundamental point to be made.

This arises from the problem of defining the boundaries for the set of test items – or the *domain* as it is called. If we had an agreed idea of what intelligence was, it would be easier to agree on what counted as an indicator of intelligence, but many disputes arise because of differing perceptions of what intelligence really is. Those who attach great importance to creativity will want to include many items in the test which test what they see as creativity. Those who see intelligence more in terms of speed and accuracy of performance will want to emphasise items which draw on tests of those skills. Each group will criticise the other for constructing an index which fails to capture adequately 'intelligence'; they will argue that it is biased. The claim of many critics, mentioned in chapter 1, that the items in IQ tests do not measure 'real' intelligence is really an argument about the appropriate domain.

Such problems do not arise in an acute form with the example of the share-price index. Everyone knows what a share is and can easily find out whether or not it is traded on the Stock Exchange. It is straightforward, in principle at least, to construct a list of such shares and to compute their average price. If we cannot handle all of them, we can easily take a representative sample. In technical language, the *population* of shares is well defined. In the case of intelligence, the population of possible test items is not at all well defined so we cannot be clear about what the population is and we certainly cannot claim that any sample of items is representative of it. It will be open to dispute whether a particular test item is legitimate or not – some might regard it as an acceptable indicator while others will not.

The mere definition of the domain, explicitly or implicitly, pre-empts the important question of what intelligence really is. It is this fact, about which critics like Rose[3] are properly concerned, that leads the cynics to dismiss the whole debate by saying that 'intelligence is what intelligence tests measure'. In effect, the whole exercise seems altogether too subjective. Intelligence becomes what we choose it to be by the tests we ask people to take. This is an inevitable weakness of IQ-like indices and is one of the reasons why their usefulness is so controversial and limited.

This point is so important that we illustrate it further by reference to a similar situation which might arise in a different context. Imagine an international athletics contest, between a group of countries, in which success is measured by the number of medals won. The number awarded to each competing country will, in the public estimation, be a measure of the athletic prowess of that country. But 'athletic prowess' measured in this way depends on the mix of events included in the contest. Adding new sports such as synchronised swimming, snooker or, even, ballroom dancing would change the meaning of 'athletic prowess' as measured by the medal tally. So would introducing a new rule to exclude competitors under twenty-five years of age. Countries which proposed such changes would be regarded warily to see whether they were trying to manipulate the rules to their own advantage. All proposals of this kind involve changing the boundaries of what constitutes national athletic achievement. The medal totals are collective properties of the outcomes and what they measure depends on which outcomes are selected. Many critics of IQ tests think that the testers behave in much the same way. They believe that, deliberately or inadvertently, they rig the tests in favour of particular groups.

'Intelligence is what intelligence tests measure'

This is a good point at which to return to the claim, mentioned in passing in chapter 1 and again here, that intelligence is what intelligence tests measure.

Defining something in terms of its own definition is properly seen as the last resort of those who have given up hope of finding a serious definition. The perceived circularity in the statement has been lampooned by, for example, the late Michael Howe (Howe 1997, p. 4).[4] Looked at more carefully it is, essentially, a statement about the crucial role played by the domain of test items. This uncertainty about the domain does not, however, justify the dismissal of IQ on the grounds that the very notion is based on a tautology.

To say that intelligence is what intelligence tests measure is an incomplete statement but it is not vacuous. The content of a battery of test items is defined by what is common to the set of items which were used to construct it. These items are not chosen haphazardly but selected to convey, as far as our crude notion will allow, what we mean by the word 'intelligence'. In a real sense, this set of items is a way of saying what we mean by 'intelligence'. The crucial question is: what does this test battery measure? The answer to this question is our provisional definition of intelligence. Intelligence, we repeat, is a collective property of the set of items. If the individual items have meaning, so does the aggregate. To say 'intelligence is what intelligence tests measure' is much the same as saying that size is what measurements of length and girth on the human body measure and athletic performance is what performance in track and field events measure.

Definition by dialogue

Choosing a domain of test items and making an appropriate selection from it is far from straightforward. We used the phrase 'our crude notion' above to emphasise that at the start of the measuring process our ideas will usually be rather vague. We suggest that this initial crude notion can be sharpened by *dialogue*.

The essence of our whole approach is that the core notion of what the word intelligence means is embedded in the language which we use. If we utter sentences containing the word *intelligence*, we presumably believe that those sentences have meaning – otherwise we would be knowingly talking nonsense! Nevertheless, as we have noted above, it is undoubtedly true that the precise meaning of the word is not fixed.[5] Different people use it in different senses though those senses may be broadly overlapping. According to the approach adopted here, the purpose of a theory of measurement is to make explicit, and to refine, what is already implicit in the common usage of the word. Our suggested approach to the construction of indices like IQ will therefore proceed through a cycle of stages, each cycle helping us to arrive at a more precise idea of what we mean. Put another way, we envisage conducting a *dialogue* between the proposed measure of intelligence on the one hand and the everyday use of the term on the other. The *measurement process* itself is therefore helping us to define exactly what we mean when we use the word intelligence. This can be set out as a formal series of steps. We make no claim that this is how current indices of IQ were, in fact, arrived at though one can trace most of the elements in the history of the subject. What follows is a rationalisation, after the event.

(1) We begin with a crude idea of what we mean by intelligence and then select some items, that is questions or tests, which we think require intelligence to find the correct answers.

(2) We construct an index (usually an average of some kind) from the responses to these items which tells us what these items have to say about intelligence as we understand it at this stage in the process.

(3) We then ask how adequately this index embodies the notion that we are trying to capture. This is essentially a subjective exercise but there are several ways in which we can introduce a little objectivity into the process. For example, we could rank individuals according to the index and ask whether the resulting ordering accords with what we would have arrived at without the help of the index. Or, we can ask whether individuals who come close together on our scale are really so similar when judged intuitively. This process may enable us to identify some items which contribute a lot to the proposed measure and others which are of rather marginal importance. If this is so, then we could delete the less good items and add others which seem to share the characteristics of the good ones. If there are serious discrepancies between the performance of the index and what we expect of it, we must cast around for items testing aspects which we appear to have overlooked. To put it fancifully, we might note that an Einstein or a Mozart would not do very well on our test and that would lead us to ask why that was, whether it mattered and, if so, what needed to be done about it.

(4) We next proceed to use this new set of items and administer the tests to a new sample of individuals and again assess the results for their subjective validity. That is, we ask how closely the values assigned to individuals match our intuitive notions of what they should be.

(5) We then continue to add, delete and modify items until we have a set with which we are satisfied.

(6) Finally, we examine whether the measuring instrument works in a wide variety of circumstances. To test whether that is so, we would apply the instrument to many different samples in many different circumstances to see whether it performs as we would expect. If it does, our object has been achieved, but if it fails we must try to identify the cause of failure and adjust the items accordingly.

The purpose of this exercise is not to eliminate subjectivity – because that is impossible – but to bring the performance of our measuring instrument into line with what we understand to be the commonly accepted meaning of intelligence. Its success would depend on the extent to which there was a common understanding of the concept. Although this still does not get us out of the wood, it does force us to clarify and, so far as possible, agree on, what we mean by intelligence. The fact that, in practice, considerable disagreements still exist indicates that this procedure is not fully adequate. It may help to refine our notion of intelligence but it will not succeed in arriving at full agreement, even when due allowance is made for ideological agendas.

To some extent the sources of disagreement can be identified and, in principle at least, reduced. The items in most IQ tests fall into groups. The Wechsler Adult Intelligence Scale, for example, includes items in groups labelled, Vocabulary, Similarities, Picture Completion and so on.[6] The argument about boundaries is therefore partly about what types of item have a place. An appropriate set of items to include in each group then becomes a secondary matter, although still an important one. But the existence of such groups raises the important question of the dimensionality of intelligence on which we shall have much more to say in chapter 8. We have already noted that there are arguments about whether there are different sorts of intelligence. If there are, one number will not be enough to express the full complexity of what is involved.

Another aspect of item choice concerns the selection of items from the domain. We want them, in some sense, to be representative. The value of the measure obtained from any particular sample of items ought to be an approximation to the value we would have obtained had we had access to, and been able to use, the whole set of items of this kind which could be constructed. This set is somewhat poorly defined and we shall have to return to the issue at a later point. In the meantime, we note that it is a potential source of dispute.

The process of dialogue advocated above offers a partial resolution of disputes about the domain. But why not enlarge the domain to include everything that any one might conceivably want to include and then winnow the resulting collection by the process of dialogue until a satisfactory index emerges? Binet, in fact, suggested something rather like this when he claimed that the content of the list of items did not matter too much as long as it was broad enough. In other words, if we cast the net wide enough we are sure to catch the items we need. If intelligence really is such a widespread and fundamental characteristic of human beings, we would certainly expect to find it turning up almost everywhere without having to look too hard! The search surely does not need to be conditioned by any prior judgement about what it is we are looking for. Our subjective judgement should then only come into play in giving a name to what we find.

Does IQ have a future?

The short answer is: no. This is not to say that IQ indices are useless – far from it. Most of this chapter has been devoted to showing how they can be given a sensible, empirical, justification. They can be criticised, however, and we have just rehearsed some of their weaknesses, in particular the arbitrariness of the domain. We have also hinted at a further difficulty arising from the dimensionality question. These are both reflections of the fact that the 'index' approach lacks an adequate conceptual framework within which issues like this can be properly formulated and resolved. In short, as we promised, we have made the best case we can for this approach but, in the last resort, it is not good enough. The argument of this book is that there is a better approach to follow which we have already traced from Spearman through the factor analysis tradition.

The foregoing discussion has not taken us along a blind alley because much of what we have said is equally relevant to use of the g-scores which we shall be advocating at a later stage. In particular, this is because of the emphasis we have placed on what the data are telling us. Our basic line, common to both approaches, is that we give priority to the data. Instead of starting with a precise definition and then asking what items we should choose in order to measure that concept, we start at the other end. We search among a large number of possible items to see whether there are those which, collectively, suggest a scale to which we can reasonably give the name 'general intelligence'. This, however, is to anticipate a conclusion which lies several chapters ahead; before that point is reached, the necessary groundwork has to be laid.

4 First steps to *g*

More about collective and individual properties

This short chapter is primarily for those who are fearful of what lies ahead and might be tempted, at this point, to turn back. Except for the title and the last line, *g* is not mentioned and there is no technical discussion at all. Instead, the aim is to show that the essence of factor analysis is already familiar to us. We do it in an informal way all the time and the purpose of the theory is, simply, to identify the key ideas and to provide the tools to carry the analysis out quantitatively.

We have already made the point that collective properties are familiar in everyday life. It will help us to get to grips with the nature of the factor analysis of mental abilities if we begin here and spend a little more time exploring this relatively familiar territory. Personality was mentioned as an example of a collective property which seems to be rather more than a simple average of a set of personal attributes. Two other, rather simpler, collective properties which lend themselves to the sort of exploratory investigation we wish to undertake are *size* and *shape*. These are familiar to all of us and yet they have a good deal in common with the more elusive and contentious matter of intelligence which is our ultimate goal.

Many objects occurring in nature vary in size and shape; pebbles on the beach, apples or, even, octopuses. The concepts of size and shape are something which we recognise intuitively. We speak quite happily about one apple being larger than another, or having a different shape, without being conscious of having based that judgement on any formal procedure. We simply look at a few specimens and immediately 'see' the variation in size and shape. If we were challenged to defend our judgement, we would no doubt point to dimensions such as height, circumference and depth in support of our claim. It is important to emphasise that we are not thinking here of regular solids like tennis balls which all share the same simple shape and which can be characterised by one measurement such as diameter. In such cases a single measurement, such as the diameter, suffices to determine the size. For a regular solid, like a brick, it is difficult to separate the notions of size and volume, which are very closely linked. Its volume is obtained by multiplying the three obvious measurements – length, breadth and height. (It is interesting to notice in passing, that it is multiplying in this case, not adding, which produces the summary measure here.) What we are really after begins to emerge when we move on to irregular things like pebbles and shells on the beach. However, these are still relatively simple objects whose size can often be adequately conveyed by just two or three measurements of length taken in various directions. The real challenge arises when we turn to more complicated objects like the human body. If we think for a moment about size, it is less easy to express our intuitive notion of size in this case by just one or two measurements; there is an almost unlimited number of measurements one could make that seem relevant. But we do recognise that people vary in size and in making such judgements we are mentally processing a large amount of information about the dimensions of the individuals in front of us.[1]

It is clear that any measurement we might make tells us *something* about overall size but that no measurement is adequate by itself. The question of measuring something like size, therefore, resolves itself into deciding what measurements to make and then finding a way of summarising the resulting information and expressing it in quantitative form in a way that it is consistent with our intuitive notion of 'size'. In other words, we are after something which will tell us what they all 'add up to'.[2] That last phrase is particularly revealing, because it shows that we already have some intuitive notion of how we might construct an overall measure of something like size.

In chapter 3 we used the humble average as an example of something which measures a collective property of a set of numbers. We have just been hinting that it might provide a measure of the size of an object. However, there is an important difference between the everyday average and the average of a set of measurements which we might contemplate using as a rudimentary measure of size. The ordinary average is a summary of a large number of measurements of the *same* characteristic on *different* objects, whereas what we are proposing summarises a large number of *different measurements* on the *same* object. Nevertheless, there is enough in common between the two procedures to give us some insight into the nature of concepts like size, so we shall ignore the distinction for the time being. In slightly more technical language, the average is a summary of a sample of measurements on a single variable; size is a summary measure (not necessarily an average) of a sample of variables.

Why stop at one collective property?

The foregoing discussion has focused on size as an example of a collective property. However, we are well aware that size is not a complete way of describing how complex objects like ourselves differ. Returning to pebbles on the beach, we can imagine sorting them into groups whose members we judge to be about the same size. Within each group we will still be able to distinguish variation, an important aspect of which will be summarised in what we call *shape*. There will be some pebbles which are nearly spherical, some flat, some sausage-shaped and so on. Shape is quite different to size but we recognise it in the same sort of way. The tall, thin person is readily distinguishable from their short, fat cousin. If pressed to explain what it was about the two that enabled us to make that distinction, we might point to the fact that 'length' measurements on the one tended to be large relative to the 'girth' measurements whereas on the other the reverse was true.

In recognising that both size and shape enter into our judgements about how people vary, we are saying that the variation we intuitively recognise is *two-dimensional* (in fact, we could, perhaps, go on to identify further dimensions). All this means is that it takes two numbers to locate one individual in relation to others. We should not, therefore, be surprised to find that the variation of human abilities, when we come to them, cannot be adequately captured by a single dimension.

In the case of both size and shape, we usually make the judgements intuitively using the eye but, as we have noticed, there are measurements which could be made on the bodies to support those judgements. It is the business of factor analysis to formalise those judgements by extracting arithmetically from a set of measurements what the eye takes in at a glance from the whole body.

Another way of saying all this is to repeat that size and shape are *collective properties* of a set of length measurements. In the same way intelligence will turn out to be a collective property of a set of test scores which may require more than one number to summarise it. (It should be added that shape is a rather more complicated thing than we have made it appear. For example, can shapes be ordered on a single scale? We do not need to go into such matters.)

Why are we interested in things like size and shape?

Why might we wish to summarise measurements in this way? In the case of size and shape, why do we do it? After all, unless there is some good reason for resorting to quantification of things like size and shape, the whole exercise has little more than academic interest in the worst sense of that much-abused word. The fact that the words exist, and are widely used, shows that the concepts are useful. Clothing manufacturers find it very convenient to classify their customers on one or two size dimensions. At the lower end of the market this is commonly done using just one dimension. Shoes, for example, come in a range of sizes. This enables the customer to specify what size of shoe they require and for the retailer to stock sizes which will cater for almost all customers. Feet cannot, in fact, be adequately described by a single size measurement, so size is commonly supplemented by what are sometimes called different 'fittings' (shapes) which depend primarily on the width of the foot.

Moving closer to one of the main examples used later in this chapter, size is relevant in organising athletic contests where performance depends, to some extent, on size. If international contests like the Olympic Games were to be overloaded with sports at which small people particularly excel then, in the tally of medal winners, countries whose people were on the small side would have, it would be claimed, an unfair advantage. A different type of example arises in the design of vehicles for public transport – how much space should be allowed for each person? It would be impractical to consider every conceivable body measurement. What is required are one or two measures which effectively summarise the key dimensions of passengers – what we call size and shape.

Are size and shape real?

This is a good point to look again at the question of whether unobservable variables like size, shape and intelligence are real. In what sense, if any, can they be said to be 'real'? Do they really exist? These are serious philosophical questions of the kind most people think can be safely left to philosophers, but here they appear to have immediate practical implications. The answers given seem crucial for the credibility of the concept. After all, if something does not exist it surely cannot influence anything else and can thus be safely ignored. An average certainly does not exist in the sense that there is any entity in the group to which we can take something, like a tape measure, and read off its value. Nevertheless, it does exist in the sense that a measure of it can be unambiguously determined from the members of the group. It tells us something which is a fixed characteristic of the aggregate though not about any individual member of it. It does exist, therefore, just as much as the elements of the group which make it up. It exists in much the same sense as a smile exists. We know what a smile is and that it can have remarkable effects on other people. Yet as a collective property of the elements which make up a face it has no existence apart from them. Lewis Carroll understood the point and expressed it memorably in the account of Alice's encounter with the Cheshire cat.[3] In Wonderland the smile can exist independently of the cat but not in the real world. When the cat goes the smile goes with it. The smile is real enough but it is a collective property of the face and cannot exist without it.

The evidence that size and shape are meaningful and useful concepts is provided by the fact that the terms have been embedded in the language for centuries and they serve a useful purpose in human discourse and action. Much the same can be said of measures of athletic ability, intelligence and unobservable variables of other kinds.

This is not quite all there is to be said on the matter but the rest must await a deeper exploration of the ideas underlying factor analysis. The sin of reification – treating something as a 'thing' which does not really exist – is a recurring theme in the debates on intelligence. Gould has been one of the most persistent critics on this score and his concerns will be addressed directly in chapter 13.

The case of athletic ability

We now move on to another example of human variation which is less contentious than human mental ability but similar to it in many ways. People vary considerably in their athletic ability. This is recognised by us all and it is not usually a source of feelings of superiority or inferiority nor is one put at any social or economic disadvantage by lacking athletic ability. This may not always have been wholly true in some English public schools, where athletic prowess has sometimes seemed to take precedence over scholastic ability but, by and large, this is a fairly neutral subject which we can discuss without raising emotional or ideological hackles.

In attempting to quantify something like athletic ability we come very much closer to the problems of measuring mental ability. Undoubtedly some people are much more athletic than others in that they tend to excel at most kinds of sports. Indicators of athletic ability are provided by the times and distances recorded in various events. It is clear that some of that variation can be attributed to body build and physiological make-up; good co-ordination, muscularity, good lungs and a healthy heart also contribute to success. However, athletic ability is more complex than that. High jumpers are almost always very tall people, sprinters are usually muscular and compact, whereas marathon runners tend to be lean. On the whole, there are also clear differences between men and women which are partly a matter of physique and this is reflected in the separation of the two in most athletic activities both on the track and field and in such sports as tennis, cricket and football. Nourishment, training and mental attitude also contribute to actual performance.

It is obvious that, even if there is something we might call *general* athletic ability, it is reasonable to suppose that athletic ability, as the term is usually used, is a *multidimensional* quantity. That is, different sports require different physical attributes; some call on speed, some on strength, some on endurance, some on co-ordination of eye and hand and so on. Any attempt to measure it must take account of this diversity.

In the Olympics, and most athletic contests, there is a distinction between track and field events, many of the former depending on moving the human body over the track as fast as possible, the latter in propelling the body or some object as far as possible. These classes of event might be thought of as identifying two important dimensions of the ability and to keep things simple we shall restrict the discussion to athletic events of this sort.

A few athletics contests include events known as the pentathlon or the decathlon, where success depends upon being able to perform well in a range of five or ten varied activities covering both track and field. These events may be thought of as contests of some 'general' athletic ability as distinct from other events which focus on one or other dimension of the ability. It is clear that this is a complicated area and it would be surprising indeed if the parallel with mental ability were exact, but there are enough features in common for the similarity to be worth pursuing. Thus, we might wonder whether, underlying all these specific abilities, there was some major dimension of variation between people which we could legitimately describe as all-round general athletic ability or whether there are distinct and unrelated abilities. Would it be meaningful, for example, first to classify people according to their general level of athletic ability and then, among people who came at the same point on that scale, distinguish among them according to their aptitude for track and field events? Put in a slightly different way, are the various special abilities things which are virtually uncorrelated with one another, or do they have something in common? When we come to consider intelligence these are some of the fundamental questions to be asked.

More examples

Quantities like size, shape and athletic ability are not, of course, particularly esoteric concepts. Indeed they are fairly typical of many important quantities which occur in social discourse. They are spoken of as though they behaved just like any other variable, although, in fact, there is no means of observing them directly. To take another example, attitudes are spoken of as though they exist in varying degrees. Individuals may be strongly in favour, weakly in favour, neutral or against a particular proposition. The answers they give to questions offering these choices provide us with some indication of where they lie on some supposed underlying scale of the attitude. In all such cases we have to make do with a set of indicators whose values we think are related more or less strongly to the more fundamental variables (attitudes) that they are designed to tap.

We have already alluded to further examples arising in economics. For example, index numbers, particularly indices of prices, are intended to chart the changes in something like the cost of living. The cost of living is not an observable variable but a collective property which we have identified to enable us to talk economically and effectively about changing levels in the collective prices of a large number of commodities.[4] Prices are attributes of commodities and we may be interested in how the general level varies across regions or countries. It is often assumed that the cost of living can be represented on a one-dimensional scale since all prices are subject to the same economic forces, but this need not be so. Weather, for example, might affect different commodities differently. All of these quantities are collective properties and many of them play an important part in decision making.

Having established that the territory to be explored is not as unfamiliar as we may have imagined, it is time to take more specific steps towards *g*.

5   Second steps to *g*

Manifest and latent variables

We are now ready to formalise some of the ideas that have been illustrated in the previous two chapters in order to lay the groundwork for our later exposition of factor analysis. We begin with the most fundamental distinction of all. It is what distinguishes *g* from IQ, but it goes much wider. It concerns the difference between what, in technical language, are called *manifest variables* and *latent variables*. A variable is any quantity which varies from one member of a population to another – height and hair colour in the case of human populations, for example. A variable is *manifest* if it is possible to observe it and to record its value by counting or by using a measuring instrument like a ruler, clock or weighing machine. Thus, any variable whose magnitude can be observed and expressed in units of number, length, time or weight is a manifest variable. A great many variables which appear in social discourse are of this kind. The idea can be extended to cover anything calculated from a set of manifest variables, like an average, for example. In that sense IQ is a manifest variable because, as we have seen, it is something calculated from manifest test scores and is, therefore, itself, observable.

Many of the most important variables arising in the social sphere *cannot* be directly observed. In some cases this is because we do not have access to them. Personal wealth would be such an example since, although it is a well-defined quantity, it might be judged too much of an invasion of personal privacy to ascertain what it is. But more often, and more importantly, they may be unobservable *in principle*. In fact, many of the more important quantities which occur in ordinary discourse are of this kind. We, nevertheless, speak of them as though they varied from one individual to another, just as if they were manifest quantities, even though there is no direct way of measuring them. Athletic ability and attitudes are two examples we have already met. Human beauty and personality, within a particular culture, are two more. We may say that some people are more beautiful than others, but there is no immediate and obvious way in which we can express such distinctions as points on a numerical scale of measurement. Radicalism and conservatism represent opposite ends of another scale which is commonly used, especially in political discussion, where we speak of one politician as being more right wing than another. In making that judgement we are not speaking of something which can be directly read off from some 'conservatometer', but we are somehow forming a judgement on the basis of a great deal that we know about that person.

Hitherto we have spoken of quantities like this as *collective properties* of their indicators. In the theory of the subject they will also be treated as variables in their own right and, because they cannot be observed, as *latent variables*. They are treated in ordinary language *as if* they were just like all other variables that can be directly observed. The question of whether they exist, or in what sense they exist, has already been raised in chapter 4[1] and, in the case of *g*, it is central to the subject of this book. Exactly what counts as *real* or *existing* is a very subtle question about which we shall have more to say later.

Models

The second key idea is that of a probability *model*. This may seem less familiar, but we regularly work with mental models even if we do not recognise the fact. If we are trying to understand the behaviour of a criminal, we may make predictions about his future actions. These will be based on assumptions we make about the effect of such things as early environmental influences, genetic disposition and past criminal record. To do this we need to have a 'picture' of the criminal in our mind. Our predictions are based on the supposition that the real person will behave like the fictitious individual we have imagined. That individual serves as our *model* of the real person. The accuracy of our predictions will depend on how closely the two correspond. A good model will do a better job than a bad one. The model may only exist in our mind or it may be written on paper or stored in a computer. The essential thing is that there shall be some correspondence between the elements of the model and its subject.

The crucial step in the factor analysis approach is to construct an adequate model for the relationships among the variables. That is, to measure intelligence we must establish a link between the manifest and latent variables (the test items on the one hand and *g* on the other). Starting with a set of manifest variables, such as test scores, we want to make some deductions from their values about the corresponding value of the latent variable which lies behind them, which here will be *g*. The idea behind this is that intelligence determines, in part at least, the values of the test scores. If that is so, we have to use the relationship between them in reverse in order to discover what intelligence score gave rise to them. The link between the latent and manifest variables which makes that possible is provided by the *model*. In this context, the model is, essentially, a formula which predicts what a test score will be if 'intelligence', however defined, has a particular value. Proceeding backwards we can then ask what the intelligence score would have had to be if the test scores are as we find them.

But how can we know what this link is? The short answer is that we cannot know, because there is no way we can observe it. If we can observe only one half of the linkage, there is no way we can know anything about the other half. This should not deter us, however. The only thing we can do is to guess what the link might be and then check retrospectively whether our guess was right. If it is not, we must make another guess. Fortunately, there is a considerable volume of experience to guide us in our choice and so narrow down the options. We will therefore proceed, for the moment, as if the link were known.

To make the situation more concrete let us think of the problem in very simple terms with just two variables. We can then picture what is going on in a way commonly used in the financial pages of newspapers. Suppose the two variables were family income and expenditure. We might imagine income playing the role of a latent variable and expenditure being the manifest variable. Our model now has to express the relationship between them. One would expect expenditure to rise as income increases so let us imagine that the relationship is as it appears in the upper part of figure 5.1. The figure shows that expenditure increases as income increases – the farther we move along the horizontal scale, the higher the corresponding value for expenditure. Using this curve we could predict expenditure for any value of income which might be given to us. This is analogous to the way in which a model for measuring intelligence would enable us to predict test scores from intelligence. Conversely, we could do things the other way round and estimate income for any value of expenditure. These two ways of using the relationship are illustrated by the arrows – at income I we predict expenditure E and *vice versa*. If the analogy holds, in the context of intelligence testing, we would expect to be able to estimate intelligence (the latent variable) given a value of the test scores (manifest variables).

Unfortunately, models are seldom as simple and deterministic as this. For a given income there will, in practice, be a range of expenditures so the position will be more like that shown in the central part of figure 5.1. Knowing a family's income, we cannot say precisely what their expenditure will be. The best we can do is to give a range, as illustrated by the upper and lower curves of the middle diagram. For an income level marked I on the horizontal scale we can say only that the expenditure is likely to lie between the two points marked as $E1$ and $E2$. In a similar way, when we try to reverse the process, to estimate income for a particular expenditure, we cannot give a precise figure but will have to settle for a range. This is shown in the lower part of figure 5.1. For an expenditure level at E, we can say only that the expected income lies in the interval from $I1$ to $I2$. The model has now become a *probability* model because it does not specify the exact relationship – uncertainty is involved.[2] Models

(i) Predicting expenditure(*E*) when income(*I*) is known and *vice versa*
for a fixed link

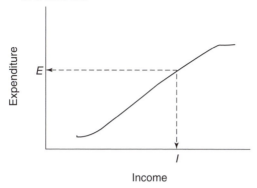

(ii) Predicting *E* from *I* when the link is uncertain

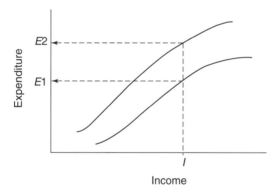

(iii) Predicting *I* from *E* when the link is uncertain

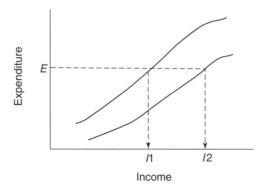

Figure 5.1 Illustrating a fixed and an uncertain link between two variables.

used to construct measures of intelligence are more like this, because there are all sorts of things which affect test scores besides intelligence.

If a satisfactory link could be found between each indicator and the corresponding latent variable (intelligence or g, say) we would have the means of converting the indicators directly into values of the latent variable. In practice, as we have noted, the situation will be more like that illustrated in the lower two parts of figure 5.1, because most indicators are contaminated, in the sense that other extraneous variables influence their value. All that we need to know about the model at the present stage of our exposition is that, given the values of the observed indicators, the mathematical technology is available to tell us, with a measurable degree of uncertainty, what value of the latent variable gave rise to them.

Variation and correlation

The ideas of variation and correlation are intimately connected and our next job must be to sort out the relationship between them. The correlations between the manifest variables may be the result of variation in latent variables; that is: variation leads to correlation. We have already met an example of how this might come about in our discussion of spurious correlation. Even if foot size and writing performance were quite unrelated in children of the same age, we saw how, in a group of mixed age, there would be a positive correlation between the two variables. One way of putting this is to say that the variation in age *induces* the correlation, because each variable depends on the common variable – age in this example. The 'third' variable which induces the correlation need not be latent, of course. Furthermore, it will often be the case that the total variation has contributions from several sources.

Thus, whenever we find variables which are correlated, it is natural to ask whether there is some variable, on which they all depend, whose variation is producing the correlation. Sometimes the 'third' variable will be obvious, or discovered fairly easily. It would not have taken much imagination to identify age as the culprit in the handwriting and foot size example. Nor would there be much difficulty in explaining the correlation between family expenditure on food and clothing in part, at least, in terms of family income. In such cases it is easy to verify any conjecture empirically. However, even if no such manifest variable can be identified, it remains open to us to identify some collective property of the manifest variables which could be thought of as inducing the correlation. It is evident that we carry out quite sophisticated mental processes when engaged in this kind of activity. Elucidating this process is, in effect, what factor analysis is all about. It attempts to mimic the mental processes by which we arrive at the concept of an underlying (latent) variable (or variables) influencing the values of a set of manifest variables.

Dimensions and dimensionality

In ordinary language, when we refer to the dimensions of an object, we usually mean its length, height and width. For things, like boxes and bricks, this is straightforward and the three figures immediately convey an impression of the overall size. For irregular things, like rocks, we can still give a fair idea of size in much the same way. The box is described as a three-dimensional object because it exists in the three-dimensional world in which we live. A rectangle drawn on paper is a two-dimensional object and a line is one-dimensional. In general we need three numbers to specify a three-dimensional object like a brick, whereas two numbers suffice for the rectangle. Dimensionality is understood in much the same way in mathematics but the idea is extended by using the geometrical language more broadly. The basic idea is to link a set of numbers with a point. Thus, for example, the scores for technical merit and artistic performance awarded in ice skating can be thought of as a point in a two-dimensional plane, like a sheet of paper. If the scores are 78 and 85 we can locate the point 78 units in the horizontal direction and 85 units in the vertical direction. For this reason we often refer to such a pair as a 'point'. By the same token, a set of scores is then represented by a cluster of points and this immediately provides us with a visual picture of their variation and correlation.

Three-dimensional variation is a little less easy to visualise but when we move up to four or more dimensions it is impossible. This need not, however, prevent us from continuing to use geometrical terminology and gaining insight from it. In this way we can think of ten scores obtained from ten items in an intelligence test as a point in ten-dimensional space. But it is because it is so difficult to 'see' the pattern in such cases that there are enormous advantages in trying to summarise the information in fewer dimensions where it is easier to, quite literally, see any pattern. Calculating an average is, perhaps, the most familiar example of reducing the dimensionality of a set of numbers, in this case, to a single dimension.

Factor analysis can be thought of as the replacement of a large number of variables (for example, test scores) by a much smaller number of latent variables which convey their essential meaning. We have been speaking, for the most part, as if this reduction to a single variable, which we hope to achieve, will lead us to something recognisable as 'general intelligence'. However, we have already seen that this may not be possible and we have chosen our language carefully to leave open the possibility that this goal may not be achievable.

Nevertheless, for measurement purposes, there are enormous advantages in being able to reduce the test variables to a single dimension. Unless we can do this, we are faced with serious problems. For example, it will not, in general, be possible to rank individuals. If, for example, we wished to select candidates for a team, and are to judge their suitability on two criteria, there may be cases where we cannot decide who should have priority. Suppose speed and endurance are both thought to be desirable for the activity in question. There is no problem in making such a ranking if individual A has better endurance and speed than individual B. The trouble arises if individual A exceeds individual B on one of the measurements but not on the other. There is then an ambiguity which cannot be resolved in a clear-cut way. If we are forced to make a ranking (as, in practice, we often are) we shall implicitly have to introduce some weighting for the measurements, that is by attaching more importance to one rather than to the other. When there are more than two characteristics on which to make the judgement, the problem is much greater. The weighting we give is, inevitably, a subjective matter and one of the aims in developing a theory is to be able to carry out this ranking in an agreed and objective way. Again, this is something which we often do unconsciously, and without recognising the subtlety of what we are doing. For example, when deciding what car to purchase we will typically take account of a large number of features, such as fuel consumption, economy, top speed, price, acceleration and so forth. Rarely do we give a precise weight to each such characteristic, but all of them are somehow taken into account in making the final judgement. Even in such everyday matters as choosing from a menu, we balance our likes and dislikes in order to arrive at a decision.

Such choices are much easier to make in a consistent fashion when we have only one quantity to pay attention to. If, therefore, we can identify some relevant single collective property of the car's attributes we can make our choice on one number alone. International comparisons of such things as unemployment, incomes and cost of living are good examples, from a different sphere, where comparisons are habitually made by reducing many-dimensional variables to a single dimension. There is, therefore, a powerful incentive for identifying a single dominant dimension of variation in any multidimensional problem. Even when this is not possible, it is better to have to contend with two or three variables than ten, say.

The measuring instrument and the measurement

Another important point to get clear from the outset is that there is a distinction to be made between the measuring instrument and the 'thing' which is measured. This is a distinction which we glossed over earlier in this chapter when we promised that there was more to be said on the question of whether latent variables exist. In their very nature, intelligence, athletic ability and all such things are unobservable. In fact, in the most literal sense, they do not exist. As we saw, they are something which we construct, but we construct them from indicators which are unquestionably real. The latent variable may be represented by a symbol in a mathematical equation which we treat exactly as if it were a manifest variable. In order to get at such a variable we construct a proxy for it.

The formula which is used to do the constructing is what we are referring to when we speak of a measuring instrument. Thus something like the retail price index is computed from a formula into which we substitute numbers (which are usually relative prices). Both the instrument and any particular number which it produces are loosely spoken of as 'the index' but they are quite distinct. Similarly, IQ and the *g*-score (an 'estimate' of *g* discussed in chapter 10) can both refer to the formula (the measurement instrument) and the number which it yields in a particular instance.

To express the difference in another way, note that the measure, in either case, is something which we can observe empirically – it is thus a manifest variable. The measuring instrument is the formula – or recipe – which we use for arriving at the index. The underlying latent variable is not observable, but we have constructed the measuring instrument in such a way as to embody the relationship which we believe to exist between the unobservable latent variable in which we are primarily interested and the indicators. A common failing in much of the literature about intelligence is the failure to discriminate adequately between these three things – namely, the underlying latent variable, the measuring instrument and the numerical value delivered by the instrument which is an 'estimate' of the latent variable. Only when these conceptual matters are quite clear can we venture into the treacherous territory of factor analysis itself.

Levels of measurement

Some types of measurement tell us more than others. The number 17, for example, might be the temperature of a liquid in degrees Celsius or it might be the weight in kilograms of a block of stone. Although the numbers look exactly the same, the amount of information which they convey depends on the context. Weights, in fact, tell us more than temperatures. In the jargon of measurement theory they represent different *levels of measurement*.[3]

To clarify this difference, we note that it is meaningful to say that a block weighing 34 kilograms is twice as heavy as one of 17 kilograms. It contains twice as much matter – it is as if there are two equal weights instead of the one. It is not true to say, however, that the liquid whose temperature is 34 degrees Celsius is twice as hot as one at 17 degrees Celsius. Why not? Is not 34 still twice 17? The short answer is that the hotter body does not have twice as much of 'something' as the other – temperature is not like matter. To explore the question a little further let us note that the units of measurement are arbitrary. The weights of the blocks can be expressed in pounds (60 lbs instead of 17 kg) but this does not alter the fact that the heavier block still weighs twice as much as the lighter. Temperature can also be expressed on various scales – Fahrenheit, for example. Seventeen degrees Celsius converts to 62.6 on the Fahrenheit scale and 34 degrees Celsius to 93.2 degrees Fahrenheit. On the Fahrenheit scale it is obvious that the second temperature is no longer twice the first.

It is clear, then, that temperature is not the same kind of thing as weight. Weight is described as a ratio level measurement because relative weights are the same whatever units we choose. Temperature is an interval level measure because intervals on the scale have the same meaning wherever they occur on that scale. For example, a shift of 10 degrees from 10 degrees to 20 degrees on the Celsius scale takes us from 50 to 68 on the Fahrenheit scale – a shift of 18 degrees. A 10-degree shift from 40 to 50 on the Celsius scale also produces the same change of 18 degrees on the Fahrenheit scale from 104 to 122. A given interval on the one scale always produces the same (but not equal) interval on the other scale no matter where it is located.

When we come to quantities like IQ or g, as we are presently able to measure them, we shall see later that we have an even lower level of measurement – an *ordinal level*. This means that the numbers we assign to individuals can only be used to rank them – the number tells us where the individual comes in the rank order and nothing else. This fact greatly restricts the use we can make of the measures and this will become apparent in later chapters when we come to deal with specific issues. It will then be very important to know what kind of operations can be meaningfully carried out on the numbers which our measurement process produces.

The stage is now almost set for the drama of factor analysis to be played out, but first we turn to the leading actor – the mysterious g.

The g-factor

At last we have got enough of the key ideas in place to broach the subject that really interests us. We now turn back to the line of development, starting with Spearman, which leads to g as a measure of general intelligence. Hitherto, g has flitted in and out of the picture as a rather ghostly entity of uncertain status. It is central to the factor analysis approach to intelligence and it is important to understand how it enters the discussion and what are its purpose and nature. There is still some way to go before a full account of g can be given but it is now possible to consolidate what we have achieved so far and to point out some of its advantages over IQ.

The idea starts, we re-call, with the empirical fact that scores on the items used in intelligence tests are mutually positively correlated. (We should not forget that this is a rather remarkable fact because it is not blindingly obvious that, for example, verbal items call on the same ability as arithmetical items.) We have noted above that, so-called, spurious correlation arises, not because two items are causally linked, but because both depend on some third factor. This makes it plausible to suppose that the mutual correlation of test items results from dependence on some unobserved source of variation. Since what the test items have in common is a requirement for effective mental activity, it follows that if there is some hidden variation among individuals it must reflect, in some degree, variation in ability to perform well on test items. If that variation were one-dimensional, we might reasonably call it 'general intelligence' and denote it by *g*. If not, we might at least hope to find a major source of variation in one dimension.

The empirical evidence, in fact, goes rather further than the observation that the correlations between test scores are positive. Some correlations turn out to be consistently larger than others and, furthermore, the variation in the size of the correlations often exhibits a systematic pattern. Verbal items, for example, tend to be more highly correlated among themselves than items drawing on different skills. This hints at the possibility that items may fall into affinity groups and hence that there may be more than one unobserved source of variation; *g* may not tell the whole story. This fact tends to count against Thomson's alternative to the idea that positive correlations could be explained by a common underlying dimension. Whilst this could explain the positivity of the correlations, it is not clear that it could be extended to account for the inequalities observed in practice. The suggestion that the latent variation may be at least two-dimensional is thus not a far-fetched speculation but a real practical possibility. If we could unravel the separate effects of several latent variables, that would be a considerable bonus.

If we could somehow isolate, or uncover, this latent variation, we would have a means of constructing a measure of general intelligence. It was Spearman's great achievement to show that this could be done and the core of this book, and the next chapter in particular, aims to show how and why, in modern terms. Spearman may not have been the originator of the name, the *g*-factor, but it is justly linked with his name.

This extremely rudimentary introduction to some of the ideas of factor analysis is already sufficient to reveal the advantages of the *g*-factor over the use of an index like IQ. First, it does not assume that intelligence is a 'one-number' quantity. It allows the data to tell us whether more than one dimension is necessary to explain the correlation among the item scores. Secondly, if there is a dominant dimension of variation, it will be revealed as such without any presupposition on our part about what it represents. This is what we meant by saying that the method allows the data to speak for themselves. In a sense, the analysis presents us with a candidate measure and leaves us to decide whether what it measures can appropriately be called general intelligence (or something else!).

What about the arbitrariness of the domain of items which we identified as one of the great weaknesses of IQ? It is true that if there is such a thing as general intelligence and if we were to exclude all items which depended on that factor, then no factor analysis could possibly discover what we had deliberately excluded. To some extent, therefore, it is still possible to manipulate the outcome by the selection of items. But if there is a *general* intelligence, it has to be widely influential, otherwise its name would be a contradiction in terms. Given a wide range of items, it would be difficult for any general ability to escape the net. Furthermore, the dialogue with the data of which we spoke, can take place in a structured way. If the same major source of latent variation emerges from the analysis whatever items are thrown into the pool, we can hardly avoid the conclusion that g has some substance. This is what has actually happened in practice.

There is one further advantage which g has over IQ which cannot be justified at this stage. This concerns, not the definition of the domain, but the selection of items from it. The actual set of items used will only be a sub-set of those that might have been used. (For example, there is a very large number of addition sums of a given difficulty which might have been selected, but only some will have actually been used.) In constructing an index like IQ we are therefore open to the criticism, voiced in chapter 3, that the result we get depends on the subjective selection of items. A different selection would have given a different IQ. The critics of IQ testing have not been slow to exploit this weakness and it is clear that they have a point. The selection question arises, of course, whatever measure we use, but the factor method enables us to assess the uncertainty generated by the fact that we have used only some of the possible items in a way that is not possible with IQ. To expound the precise reasons for this would take us into very deep inferential waters but we shall come back to the point in chapter 10.

There are still unanswered questions about how we can recognise, for example, that two factors, arising from different sets of test items, are the same g but these can be set on one side for the moment.

A dual measure?

The indicators, we have claimed, are indicators of g. The reason they are correlated is because they are all supposed to depend on g and, perhaps, on other latent variables as well, But what, exactly, *is* g? We have called it a latent variable and later we shall see that it is treated just like any variables that we can observe. All that we can say, on the basis of the foregoing discussion, is that what we observe is no different from what it would have been if there was a real, measurable quantity out there. However, so far, we are only justified in behaving *as if* g existed; in actual fact, it is only a construct – a useful fiction.

The discussion, up to this point, may seem to have an unreal feel about it, because we all think we know what is really behind the answers people give to items in intelligence tests. It may have seemed perverse to have dwelt so long on 'constructs' and 'collective properties' while ignoring the rather obvious fact that, whatever else these indicators 'indicate', they certainly reflect physical processes going on in the brain. Any summary measure we construct from them will inevitably be some kind of measure of brain performance. What a subject writes down on a piece of paper in answer to a test item is a result of a process going on in the brain. Although we may choose to regard it as a measure of this rather abstract thing called '*g*', it is also measuring a physical process. It should therefore be possible to find variations in brain structure or functioning which correspond, at least approximately, to the scores that the subjects obtain in tests. Is *g*, therefore, not better thought of as a summary measure of what goes on in the brain when a person responds to test items? Or, to use our own terminology, is *g* not really a collective property of brain function? Spearman certainly seems to have thought along these lines when he spoke of mental 'energy' or 'power'.[4]

There has been a good deal of research to identify brain characteristics or processes which can be reliably linked to performance.[5] Brain size, whether measured crudely in terms of volume, or more subtly in terms of richness of neuronal connections might, one would suppose, be a relevant indicator. Additionally, the speed or efficiency of brain processes measured, for example, by response times should be another fruitful source of underpinning for the hypothesis that *g* measures a fundamental property of the brain. There is certainly a good deal of experimental evidence pointing in this direction but, so far, its strength falls short of what is really needed.

The only point we wish to make at this stage is that our indicators are, at the same time, telling us about both performance on the test items and a property of the brain to which they are closely linked. If this is so, *g* might properly be described as a dual measure.

These things are mentioned at this point to hint at why we need something more fundamental than an intuitively based IQ index in order to get to grips with the subtlety of intelligence. The merest suggestion that we need to develop a theory may well raise hackles. It seems to suggest taking a step in the direction of abstraction when what is needed is a generous dose of reality. If there is so much dispute about IQ which, after all, seems a fairly comprehensible idea, how will things be helped by the introduction of an abstraction like *g*? Actually it is the first step out of the morass.

The theory which underlies intelligence testing may, indeed, seem remote and difficult. There is no doubt that it draws upon the more technically demanding of statistical ideas. As we shall see, even such a master of exposition as Gould confessed to finding that an exposition of factor analysis was no easy task. However, in essence, it is no more than an attempt to formalise what most of us do informally all the time.

Back to definitions

This is an appropriate point to return, yet again, to the question of definition and especially to the alleged tautological claim that intelligence is no more than what intelligence tests measure. However, this time we do it armed with new terminology and a broader framework within which to view the matter. We are dealing with a network of inter-related variables called the model. Some of those variables are manifest, others are latent. The methodology enables us to express, probabilistically, any latent variable in terms of some, perhaps all, of the manifest variables. The latent variable thus provides a way of summarising the values of the relevant manifest variables. It is as real as they are, and it takes its meaning from them. Although we choose the set of indicators on which the methodology does its work, it is the technique itself which 'decides' which to include and what weight to give them. The problem is then to decide what those manifest variables share and it is this collective property which we have to name. The meaning derives from the items, we repeat, and is no less real than they are. At the risk of appearing unduly repetitious we might add to the examples already given in chapter 3 by saying that the definition is no more tautologous than saying that the cost of living is no more than what prices measure or that weather is no more than what rainfall, temperature and suchlike measure. In reality, in the case of cost of living and weather, the criticism overlooks the fact that prices or meteorological readings are meaningful in themselves. It is the fact that they all have something in common which enables us to identify and extract what *is* common. Therefore, if we are asked what intelligence is, we look at those tests of mental ability which our theory finds 'hang together' and ask what it is that *they* have in common.

In this chapter we have, very tentatively, used some half-formed glimpses of factor analysis to get our bearings in the long trek towards an understanding of g. In the next chapter we must get to grips with the core of the matter, but without crossing the border into the realm of mathematics.

6   Extracting g

The strategy

If we have a set of test scores which are mutually positively correlated, we have argued that they may share something in common. This 'something' we have tentatively identified with g (although we have recognised the possibility that g might not be the only common influence). The question now is how to separate out what is common from what is peculiar to each test score. In mining terms we have a considerable quantity of ore which we know contains gold and we have to find a technique for separating the one from the other. Pursuing the metaphor, it is natural to speak of this process as 'extracting' g, though 'exposing' g would be more accurate in some respects. Factor analysis is the tool for carrying out the extraction. Lest this way of speaking raise false expectations, we should make clear at the outset that the metaphor is imperfect and that it may not be possible to extract g in anything like a pure form.

Factor analysis is not an elementary method and we shall make no attempt to give anything approaching a technical account. However, it is necessary to have some insight into how it works and what it can achieve. We shall adopt a threefold approach, each giving a different angle, with the intention that each will complement the others.

The first, which we have called an informal approach, is not really factor analysis at all but it may be thought of as a half-way house containing the seeds of some of the key ideas. The second, based on the latest theoretical approach, concentrates on the central idea. The third is a more traditional approach, having recognisable affinities with Spearman's original method. Taken together these different avenues get us somewhere near our destination.

An informal approach

It is useful to begin by asking how we make this extraction informally, because we often perform such an exercise without thinking of it in those terms. To take, perhaps, the simplest case, imagine that we have a student who takes a series of test items which are marked right or wrong. If we adopt the convention that a right answer scores one and a wrong answer zero, then there would usually be little argument about regarding the sum of those ones and zeros, in other words the total number correct, as the best estimate we could make of where that individual stands on the scale of ability. This has been the practice of teachers for generations. Someone who scored 9 would certainly be regarded as better than someone whose score was only 7. Furthermore, we would recognise that if there were only four items, say, the total score would be a rather imprecise measure. A moment of forgetfulness which reduced a potential score of three to two would amount to a reduction in scale position from the 75 per cent to the 50 per cent point. Few of us would wish to defend either of those numbers as a very precise figure. On the other hand, if there were fifty test items, we would feel that the vagaries of the moment would tend to balance out in this longer series. It is true that candidates might make one or two silly mistakes, or by good fortune, happen to guess one or two items correctly that they did not know anything about, but these would only produce minor perturbations in the total score. We might call this the 'swings and roundabouts effect'. In short, we would feel a good deal happier in regarding the percentage out of 100 test items as an estimate of the subject's position rather than the same percentage based on only four or five items.

Let us take a further step by supposing that, instead of having test items which are scored one or zero, we now have items where a score is given on some continuous scale. This happens, for example, when we assign a mark out of 20 or 100 as is often done in marking the work of students. Once again, suppose that we have a set of such items and that each is marked on the continuous scale from 0 to 100 so that the number we record for each can be treated as if it were an ordinary percentage. It then seems reasonable to use the total, or average, score to indicate the ability of an individual. As in the previous example, the more items we have, the more confident we feel about the answer at which we arrive. In this case we can give a somewhat more precise account of what we expect to achieve when we add up the scores. We have recognised that the individual score is subject to a degree of uncertainty. There is uncertainty arising on the part of the person tested and on the part of the person who marked the item. No one would want to argue that the figure given was a precise measure of ability when viewed from either side. It could easily have been a little more or a little less. But the error, either upwards or downwards, would not be expected to show a systematic bias in one direction or the other. In the process of adding up the scores for the individual items, we would therefore expect some to be over-estimates and others to be under-estimates and so in the process of addition there will be some balancing out. The more items we have the better the chance that this cancelling-out process will produce a balance somewhere near zero. That is the rationale behind what we feel, almost instinctively, to be a reasonable procedure – namely, that in adding up test scores we get somewhere near a measure of true ability.

What we have described implies, in effect, a very simple *measurement model*. Making things a little more formal, we can express it by saying that we have treated the score assigned to a particular test item as if it were the sum of two parts. The first part we might call the common part or the 'true score' and the second part the 'error' or 'deviation'. Thus:

Observed test score = true score + deviation.

If the deviations tend to be haphazardly positive or negative, then in a reasonably long series they might be expected to balance out. What we are left with is the true score. The averaging process can therefore be seen as a way of extracting the gold from the ore. The dross is discarded and the true score, or something close to it, remains.

This procedure is satisfactory as far as it goes, but it does not go far enough. In adding up percentage marks we are adding up the same kind of thing – numbers that are comparable because they are measured on the same scale in the same interval. But suppose that different items are measured on different scales. Some, we may suppose, are marked out of 100, others out of 20 and some, maybe, out of 10. If we simply add them up as they stand, we are implicitly giving greater weight to those items which are marked out of the larger number. Typically it would take ten items marked out of 10 to produce a score comparable with one item marked out of 100. In order to decide whether this is what we want, we have to consider whether the maximum number of marks for each item reflects the *importance* which we wish to attach to each. Does it, for example, require ten times as long to do? Or is it, in some sense, ten times more difficult? This is a subjective judgement and there is no theoretical way of providing an answer within the framework we have adopted so far. Only if we think all of the items are of equal importance is it sensible to require them all to carry the same weight in arriving at the final score. Equal weights are often assigned implicitly by first converting scores to percentages and then giving them equal weight. This is a perfectly satisfactory procedure but in deciding to use it to we have made an important subjective assessment about the relative importance of the items.

Sometimes a similar situation arises when item scores do not fall within a common range as percentages do. They might for example be response times, the idea being that the lapse of time to respond to an item is a measure of how confident one is in the answer, or how competent one is at arriving at the answer. In such cases, where the range is not fixed, there is no simple scaling of the kind we considered above which puts all the item scores on an equal footing. In such cases we have to find some other way of bringing them into line. One way of doing this is to arrange for them to have the same degree of variability. There are many ways of measuring variability, but one of the commonest is to use something called the standard deviation. If we use the standard deviation as our unit of measurement, then all scores will, of necessity, have the same variability. Such scores are said to be *standardised* and we can then add them up in exactly the same way as before – and with the same proviso about the arbitrariness of what we are doing.

Of course, we may not wish to give every item the same weight. Some items might be judged to have particular significance in revealing a person's ability. Past experience, for example, may have demonstrated that one particular item is unusually good at discriminating between individuals near the top or bottom of the range. In such cases we can, of course, give those items greater weight when we come to do the adding up, that is, by using a weighted average rather than a straight average. The extra subjectivity which this procedure introduces lays us open to the charge that we are manipulating the data and thus undermining the credibility of the whole exercise. The weighting is not the only arbitrary feature of this method of separating the dross from the gold. Although it seemed perfectly sensible to add up scores, weighted or not, this is not the only way of combining them. We could have multiplied them together, for example (see again the discussion in note 2 in chapter 4).

This leads us to ask whether there is any statistical means by which we can resolve such questions. If so then, in a manner of speaking, we would be allowing the data to speak for themselves. Fortunately, this is just what factor analysis and related latent variable methods are designed to do.

Sufficiency: a key idea

The central idea behind this section is very simple. It lies at the heart of factor analysis from whichever angle it is approached. It is a direct consequence of the proposition that mutually positive correlations between a set of variables may arise from their common dependence on a latent variable. From this it follows that, if it were possible to identify a sub-set of individuals who were at the same point on the latent scale, the correlations would disappear because we would have removed the variation which is the source of their inter-dependence.[1] Very roughly, therefore, factor analysis is an exercise in finding a latent scale such that individuals at the same point on that scale show no correlation. (Note that, for simplicity, we speak of a single latent variable but there could be several.) The technical apparatus can be regarded as a structured way of searching for such scales.

One way of approaching this problem is to think of what other things individuals at the same point on the latent scale might have in common. Taking our cue from the previous discussion it might seem sensible to group together individuals having roughly the same total score. After all, intuition suggests that those with the same total have done equally well. If that guess were right, individuals with the same total would be at the same scale point, and so there would be nothing to induce correlation among their scores.

Repeating this argument in slightly different language, the original reason for supposing that there was some common latent variable underlying our item responses was that the responses were mutually correlated. We interpreted the tendency of one response to be positively correlated with another as an indication that both owed their mutual correlation to their dependence upon a common underlying variable. Conversely, the absence of any such correlation would be indicative of no common underlying factor. Ideally, therefore, to check for the presence of an underlying variable we would want to take groups of individuals such that all members of the same group had the same value of the underlying variable and then see whether the correlation had vanished. Obviously we cannot do this because latent variables are, by definition, unobservable. The next best thing would be to find some *statistic* which we had good reason to believe was a satisfactory substitute for the latent variable and fix that instead. Here we use the term *statistic*, in the singular, to refer to any quantity we calculate from a set of observed responses, like the sum or difference between the largest and the smallest members, for example. But how could we possibly know whether we had such a statistic? The answer lies in the notion of sufficiency.

To put this intuition on a firmer footing we must explain the notion of *sufficiency*. At first sight this does not seem to have much in common with trying to make correlations vanish, but the connection will appear shortly. Sufficiency is a term used by statisticians and it has a precise technical meaning which is very closely allied to its everyday use. A statistic is said to be sufficient for *g*, say, if it contains all the information which the sample contains about *g*. In effect this means that nothing would be lost if the sample were thrown away as long as we retained the sufficient statistic. But how can we discover any such sufficient statistic and how can we tell when we have found one?

Suppose then that we have some statistic, like the sum, which is a candidate for being described as sufficient. How could we tell whether it is or not? Imagine that we were able to take a very large sample of members from the population in which we are interested and that, for each member of that sample, we calculated the sum of their scores. We could then divide the sample members into groups in such a way that all the members of any one group had the same value of the sum. (If the responses were discrete, as in the case of binary responses, this could be done exactly; if the responses are continuous we should have to group individuals whose sums were not precisely equal but close together.) If we now examine the correlations between the item responses for all those in a particular group who have precisely the same sum, we can ask whether the mutual correlation has disappeared or whether some is still present. If some degree of correlation remains, we might infer that there is still something more to be extracted from the data than is captured by the sum, which is the same for all members of this group. If, on the other hand, the correlation had entirely disappeared, the search is ended and we need invoke no further latent variable. In that case we would describe the sum as sufficient because, when its value is known, there is nothing further that the data can tell us about the common source of variation. The sufficient statistic is here behaving exactly like the supposed latent variable. Once we know its value there is nothing more the data can tell us about the latent variable.

It would, of course, be an extremely tedious and lengthy process to discover sufficient statistics by trial and error in this manner. Each attempt would involve calculating the chosen statistic for each member of the sample, classifying the members of the sample into groups having a common value of that statistic and then examining the relationship within each group. What we need is some mathematical method which will automatically uncover such a sufficient statistic, if one exists. There is no guarantee, of course, that a sufficient statistic will exist, and unless there is one, the approach we are describing will not be of much use. Here, again, theory comes to the rescue and is able to tell us under what circumstances this sufficient reduction of the data to a single statistic can be achieved. For the moment we merely mention that it can frequently be done and in such cases the sufficient statistic often turns out to be either a simple sum or, more likely, a weighted sum. In cases when it cannot be done we may be able to get tolerably close to the ideal.[2]

An embarrassment of solutions!

The possibility of finding a sufficient statistic seems to solve, in principle at least, the difficult problem with which we started. Having to find a suitable measure for an underlying variable reduces to the problem of discovering some statistic having the property that, when it is constant, all mutual correlations disappear. This statistic can then be regarded as a substitute for the latent variable. This is fine as far as it goes but a moment's reflection reveals a worrying ambiguity. Let us imagine that we have discovered that the sum of the item responses is sufficient. It immediately follows that three times the sum, or three times the sum with ten added, will also be sufficient; for if the sum is sufficient then multiplying by three and adding ten does not change anything that matters – those grouped together because they had the same sum will remain together because they now have the same transformed value. There is nothing to prevent any intending user from making any transformation of this kind.

It hardly seems satisfactory that two investigators should arrive at different measures. In technical language we are saying that the zero point and units used for the measurement scale which we have constructed are quite arbitrary. There is nothing in the data which allows us to prefer one choice over another. However unfortunate this seems, it is a fact of life and brings to light a fundamental limitation on what we are trying to do. But worse is to come!

The argument does not have to be restricted to simple changes of zero point and units such as we have just considered. Other versions of the sufficient statistic can be generated by other kinds of transformation. For example, if the sufficient statistic turns out to be the sum and if that sum is necessarily positive, then the logarithm of the sum is also sufficient – when one is constant, so is the other. The logarithmic and linear scales are very different in terms of the spacing they give to individuals on the scale. Yet apparently there is nothing in the data which allows us to prefer one scaling over the other. In fact, to use technical language again, any one-to-one transformation of the statistic will retain the property of 'containing all the relevant information'.

The point can be made more clearly, perhaps, in relation to a very simple numerical example. Suppose that we have arrived at a score for six individuals based on a sufficient statistic as follows:

Ann	Barry	Carol	Desmond	Elsie	Fred
10	17	21	24	32	35.

Instead of using these scores someone proposes to multiply them by 2 and add 3. The scores, in the same order, now become:

23	37	45	51	67	73.

If, instead, we square the original scores we obtain:

100	289	441	576	1024	1225.

According to our reasoning each of these scorings is equally good, yet the magnitudes of the numbers, and their spacings, are very different. However, one important feature does not change from one case to another and that is the rank order. Whichever set we take, the individuals are placed in the same order. In effect we are saying that the approach we are following only permits us to *rank* individuals on the latent dimension. Anything beyond that represents a subjective addition to the data and must be recognised as such. We are entitled to adopt whichever set of scores we like, as long as we make it clear that the particular spacing we have chosen is arbitrary. Fortunately, a great deal can be done with the ranks alone.

Thus it appears that there is no empirical way of producing a unique scale for any latent variable uncovered in this way. Whether or not this is a good thing is a question we shall have to come to grips with shortly. However it is immediately clear that, if the data can take us no farther than this, we are not going to be able to provide definitive answers to some very important practical questions. It also places a serious question mark against many things which are part of the stock in trade of the IQ industry. First among these is the distribution of g.

The whole idea of something like intelligence being normally distributed is cast into doubt. For, if we were to offer our sufficient statistic as a measure of intelligence, someone might come along and point out that the square of this quantity had just as strong claims to be considered. If one of these quantities were normally distributed it is obvious that the other could not be. If there are an unlimited number of possible measures, it is also clear that we can say nothing about the distribution of the underlying latent variable to which they are supposed to be related. It is, indeed, true that we can make no empirically justifiable statement about the form of the distribution of a latent variable.

The description we have just given is not a recipe for doing factor analysis and nor is it a completely accurate or complete account of what factor analysis actually does. Readers familiar with Gould's account, to which we come in chapter 7, may be at a loss to relate anything said above either to this, or other traditional expositions. Nevertheless, our account aims to capture the essence of the ideas underlying it in a manner which exposes some of the arbitrariness which is involved. It may help, therefore, to recapitulate the main steps as follows:

(1) If a set of test scores tend to be positively correlated among themselves there is a *prima facie* case for believing that those correlations are induced by a common dependence on a latent variable.

(2) If we can find sub-sets of the population of individuals, defined by having common values of a sufficient statistic, such that the mutual correlations have virtually disappeared within those sub-sets, we conclude that, within those groups, the latent variable does not vary.

(3) Those sub-sets then must correspond to different points on the scale of the latent variable which induced the original correlations in the complete population.

(4) However, it is only the order of those points which has meaning.

If the first two conditions are met, we have found evidence for the existence of a single latent variable, which in the present context, would be identified as g. Furthermore, we have determined scores which enable us to rank individuals according to where they come on the scale of g. None of this should be taken to imply that it is always possible to find a sufficient statistic or that, if we can, that it will be one-dimensional. All that we are saying is that if all this can be done, and it often can, then certain things follow.

The classical approach

Neither of the foregoing approaches bears much resemblance to what you will find in most elementary text book treatments of factor analysis. Nevertheless, it is important to emphasise again that both encapsulate key ideas which are important for evaluating the claims and counter-claims of the protagonists in the IQ debate. Now, however, it is time to turn to something more traditional, in the spirit of Spearman and the early pioneers. First we give a brief outline intended to set out a general idea of the rationale behind the method; then we fill in some of the detail for readers able to cope with a slightly more technical treatment. Before going on it would be worth looking again at the 'Models' section of chapter 5 (especially the discussion of figure 5.1) where the idea was given a first outing.

As so often happens in applied mathematical work, the way to get started is to pretend that we already know something that is actually unknown. It may then turn out to be unnecessary or, perhaps, much less important than we imagined. In the present case the chief obstacle is that any latent variable is unknown and unknowable. Let us begin by treating it as if it were an observable one-dimensional variable. If it were, life would be much easier for we could then check directly whether or not it was wholly, or partly, responsible for the observed correlations among the manifest variables.

A rough and ready way of doing this would be to plot each manifest variable, in turn, against the latent variable exactly as illustrated in figure 5.1. Once we knew that these relationships existed, we could describe them mathematically. Such descriptions would involve unknown quantities determining the strengths of the relationships. For example, if the plots suggested straight line relationships, these quantities would be the slope of the line (measuring the strength of the relationships) and the intercept (the point at which it cuts the vertical axis). From these descriptions we could go on to deduce mathematical expressions for the correlations. Then, by equating these predicted values to the actual values, we could infer what the unknowns in the original relationships (e.g. the slopes) would have had to be to yield these particular correlations. This does not provide us with values for the unobserved latent variable, but it does enable us to predict what their values would be for any given set of test scores. This is possible because we have indirectly estimated the relationships between the manifest variables and the latent variable. By inverting these relationships we can then say something about the latent variable, given the manifest variables.

If we cannot adequately explain the observed correlations by using one latent variable in the way just described, we could go on to introduce a second latent variable, and so on.

Before we can develop these ideas further it will be helpful to make a historical digression. There was a marked change in the way that statisticians conceptualised what they were doing which can be traced roughly to the period following the Second World War. At around that time statisticians began to routinely start their investigations by formulating a probability model for the processes they were about to study. This is crucial for our purposes because it marks the transition to the old way of looking at factor analysis, in which critics like Gould were schooled, the modern approach.

To convey the idea let us take a very simple example. Suppose we draw a random sample of 100 people from the population of a town and ask each of them whether or not they were born in that town. This will tell us, maybe, that 74 (that is 74 per cent) of the sample were natives. But what we really want to know is what that figure would be if we had been able to ask every inhabitant. The question which model-based inference is designed to answer is: what can we infer from the sample about the whole population? The model specifies how the sample values are related to those of the population and hence provides a bridge from sample to population. That bridge is probabilistic because the (random) method of sampling enables us to calculate how likely we are to obtain a particular sample in terms of the characteristics of the population. By inverting the logic of the argument we can hope to say something probabilistically about the population. For example, how far the true proportion of native-born residents is likely to be from the sample value of 74 per cent.

Taking this further, to bring it a little closer to factor analysis, consider the relationship between annual income and annual savings in such a population. We might expect that the more people earned, the more they would save. In this case we know savings would have to come out of what was left after basic living expenses had been met so we might expect savings to go up in proportion to income above some basic minimum. We might guess that:

savings = a fixed proportion of (income − basic expenses).

To be realistic, we have to allow that other factors will play a part and blur this simple relationship. To accommodate this we add a 'catch-all' term to the right-hand side. This so-called 'random error' or 'residual' will vary from one person to another and so it is best thought of as a probabilistic quantity with a specified frequency distribution. What we now have is a *model* – actually what is known as a regression model.[3] It enables us to predict how much someone will save if we know what their income and basic expenses are. In order to make the model usable we need to know the fixed proportion of surplus income which is saved. The analysis is then directed to determining these two unknowns – the proportion and the basic expenses. Neither of these quantities is directly observable, so their values have to be inferred from the data available to us. Once these unknowns have been estimated we can use the equation in various ways. Given someone's income we could predict their savings. The converse is to estimate income given savings. It is in this second mode that we come nearest to factor analysis.

In the case of factor analysis the position is similar though a little more complicated. The first attempt to bring factor analysis into the mainstream of statistical theory was made by Lawley and Maxwell in 1963 in a small but influential book called *Factor Analysis as a Statistical Method*.[4] Factor analysis, we recall, aims to discover whether the mutual correlations between a set of manifest variables – the test scores – can be explained by their common dependence on a smaller set of underlying, unobservable or latent variables. In the context of intelligence testing the items will have been selected on the supposition that they depend on some underlying variable which characterises the mental capacity of the individual. This, it is supposed, varies from one individual to another. This assumption does not preclude dependence on other latent variables, but if the items are well chosen there should be one dominant dimension of latent variation (see chapter 8 for more on this). We therefore need a model which links the values of the test scores to the assumed underlying variable on which they principally depend. This will, inevitably, have to include some random error terms because it would be naïve to suppose that test scores were wholly determined by the latent variables. The standard model, known as the normal linear factor model, is rather like the regression model used as an example above. It supposes that the score on each test item is a linear combination of any latent variables – ideally only one – plus a random error term.

On that assumption we can predict what the correlations ought to be and hence see whether they correspond with those we have actually observed. If the correspondence is close, we can say that the data are consistent with the hypothesis that the observed correlations were generated in the manner specified by the model.

Item response theory

Almost all presentations of factor analysis start from the idea of correlations between variables. We have also used this approach when building on the key idea that positive correlations among a set of variables point to a common, underlying, latent variable which induces these correlations.

Unfortunately, many of the manifest variables which arise in intelligence testing, and similar applications, are not the sort of variables which lend themselves to the calculation of correlations. Many are binary – that is they take two values – right/wrong or true/false, for example. Binary variables are the simplest kind of *categorical* variable. A more complicated version places responses in one of several categories. These are called *polytomous* variables. For example, we may classify responses to an attitude question as: strongly agree, agree, no opinion, disagree, strongly disagree. In such cases we have no numbers from which we can calculate correlations. What, then, are we to do? One very common solution is to arbitrarily assign numbers to the categories. Thus binary variables can be coded 0 or 1. The categories of polytomous variables, such as the attitude response, could be labelled, $-2, -1, 0, 1, 2$ or, perhaps, $-5, -2, 0,$

2, 5. The arbitrary nature of this latter assignment should make us feel uneasy because we are adding something to the data. The correlations resulting from such an exercise are not the sort of correlations that factor analysis is designed to deal with. The results may be almost meaningless.

Great ingenuity has been shown in devising ways of measuring the strength of the relationships between such categorical variables by pseudo-correlation coefficients so that standard factor analysis can be applied. This is now unnecessary practically, and superfluous conceptually. The treatment given under 'sufficiency' above covers all kinds of variables with one minor change in terminology. We spoke of correlation between variables because this is the familiar term. It would have been more accurate to have spoken of dependence and independence, which are the fundamental concepts. Correlation is a way of measuring dependence under certain conditions. We have used the term generically. What really matters, for example, is that when we condition on a sufficient statistic, the items should be independent.

A better way forward is to use a *model* specifically designed for the data we have, rather than to try to force categorical data into an inappropriate mould. For this purpose there is something known as *item response theory* (IRT). This starts from the common testing situation in which all our indicators, or manifest variables, are binary (usually, in this context, right/wrong). It is supposed that these all depend on a single underlying factor (or, *trait*, as it is often called). From this starting point one can develop methods exactly parallel to those of factor analysis. One might reasonably describe them as *factor analysis for binary data* though it is more limited than factor analysis in that it only allows one factor. Many extensions of basic IRT methods have been made, in particular to polytomous response variables. This approach does not start from correlations but from the collection of response patterns, but its aims and objects are nevertheless exactly the same.[5]

Item response theory is not merely very similar to factor analysis, in essence it is the same as factor analysis. More accurately both factor analysis and item response theory are special cases of something which is called the *generalised linear latent variable model*.[6] We do not need to elaborate further on this beyond noting that there is a more general way of looking at these problems which has considerable practical benefits. The non-technical account we have given in this chapter aims to capture the essence of this more general approach and shows, incidentally, that correlations are not at the heart of factor analysis. They are simply intermediate quantities which happen to arise in the course of the calculations when the manifest variables are continuous. The core of the method lies in using a model in which all manifest variables are linked to one or more latent variables (such as g).

This broader perspective, and the developments associated with it, seems, so far, to have largely escaped the notice of the psychometric community which is much more comfortable with the well-tried, if sometimes inappropriate, methods of traditional factor analysis. Until this isolation is ended, the simplifying and powerful concepts on which the modern statistical modelling of latent variables is based will fail to make their contribution to the measurement of intelligence.

This is an appropriate point to mention a further term which is sometimes used in the intelligence testing community, namely 'test theory'. The distinctions between factor analysis, item response theory and test theory have more to do with differing research communities and their traditions than with the basic ideas. At the level of the present treatment, everything is covered by the term factor analysis.

Some practical issues

Our discussion of extracting *g* represents one extreme of the spectrum of types of explanation one could give of factor analysis (informal and non-mathematical). At the other extreme lies the computational method. Software packages are widely available for carrying out the analysis. All that they require in the way of input are a few numbers – often correlation coefficients. They will then produce a dazzling array of outputs in graphical and numerical form. It is so easy that virtually anyone can carry out factor analysis and the social science literature is full of such analyses, usually given with little background and interpreted with scant regard for the assumptions and uncertainties on which the results depend. In fact, the simplicity of it all is so seductive that there is a strong temptation to massage the problem until it fits the Procrustean bed of one of the standard packages. If such packages call for input in the form of correlation coefficients, then correlation coefficients must be provided whether or not they are appropriate or meaningful. It is tempting to deliver an extended homily on the evils of the incorrect application of factor analysis but this must be resisted.

The reader now has a choice. One is to continue with the next chapter which looks critically at an alternative, closely related, treatment of the same topic as this chapter, given by Gould in *The Mismeasure of Man*. The alternative is to proceed directly to chapters 8, 9 and 10 which complete our account of factor analysis.

7   Factor analysis or principal components analysis?

What is principal components analysis?

This chapter is a digression to look at a competitor to factor analysis. It is a competitor in much the same sense as the baby cuckoo in the nest. To many people it looks much the same but it is actually a different kind of animal. The confusion between the two methods arises from the numerical similarities. In both, the input consists of correlation coefficients and the output is in much the same form. In fact, at least one of the major software packages treats principal components analysis as one of several versions of factor analysis, and so the output comes in exactly the same form. Yet, conceptually, there are fundamental differences.

So what is principal components analysis (hereafter, PCA) and why is it relevant to intelligence testing?[1] It is a method which yields an index, not unlike an IQ measure, which is a weighted average of test scores. What makes it special is the way in which the weights are chosen. It goes farther than the typical method of constructing an IQ measure in that the weights are determined by the data and not prescribed in advance. The idea is as follows. If all the test scores are indicators of 'intelligence', they will vary, partly because the individuals on which they were measured vary in intelligence, and partly for other reasons irrelevant to the main object. The object is to find a measure which discriminates as effectively as possible between individuals of differing intelligence. Thus the more an index varies, the better discriminator it will be. The aim is to choose the weights to be applied to the test scores so as to maximise the variation. This produces what is known as the first principal component. Having calculated the measure, we may go on to ask what it appears to be measuring, in exactly the same way as for any other index. In practice, with a representative collection of test items, the first component turns out to be much what we would expect for a measure of general intelligence. Many writers call this index g but this is misleading. As we have defined it, g is an unobservable characteristic of the individual, not an index. The value of the principal component obviously depends on which particular items happen to be selected and on all the uncertainties of measurement associated with the test items.

The major practical difference is that principal components analysis is applicable only when the variables are continuous, so it cannot be used if some of the variables are categorical.[2] It requires a set of correlation coefficients as its starting point. The reason that it is so closely associated with factor analysis is that, under the typical circumstances one meets in intelligence testing, PCA provides a good approximation to factor analysis.[3] When applicable, therefore, it is best regarded as a numerical approximation to factor analysis, valid when the test scores permit the calculation of correlation coefficients as measures of dependence. Much of what we wish to say about the use of PCA will emerge from a critique of Gould's exposition of factor analysis through the medium of principal components analysis. To this we now turn.

Gould's version

We have seen that in order to understand fully the debates about g, one must understand the technique of factor analysis on which much of the argument depends. Our exposition, given in chapter 6, has aimed to provide such an understanding. Gould also recognised the need for an elementary exposition and, in his book, *The Mismeasure of Man* (Gould 1996) he undertook to give a plain guide to the subject for the uninitiated. This was an ambitious, but worthwhile attempt, since popular accounts of the topic are sadly lacking. He did not entirely succeed and the purpose of this section is to expose the inadequacies of his treatment. These turn out to be crucial for understanding what g really is. The publication of *The Bell Curve* in 1994 provided the opportunity for Gould to issue a second edition of his book and, in the process, to give his reaction to some of the criticisms which had been made of the first edition. These are particularly illuminating, especially as they relate to his account of factor analysis.

Gould's book seems to have been welcomed with great enthusiasm by the popular press but the reception accorded by the professionals was more equivocal. This is hardly surprising since one easily gets carried away by the sheer exuberance and zest of the writing. It is natural, if not always wise, to suppose that he who writes well, also writes with authority. There were, however, many criticisms of his treatment but they can really be boiled down to two. First, that Gould, as a palaeontologist, was presuming to teach others a subject on which he, himself, was not an expert. Secondly, that he was using his exposition as a vehicle for the propagation of left-wing anti-hereditarian views.

Gould's response to these criticisms is particularly interesting and forthright. To the first he replied, essentially, that he *was* an expert on factor analysis, more so than many psychologists, because it was the technique which he had used in his doctoral research and some of his early publications. In addition to this he pointed out that he did his early research at a time when he was enthusiastic about the application of statistical and computational techniques in his field of study and, in consequence, he had spent a year studying the technique. In short, he claimed to be more expert than many of his critics. Further, for good measure, he fended off further criticism with a withering attack on the small-mindedness of those who make such criticisms. 'The saddest parochialism in academic life . . . lies in the petty sniping that small-minded members of one profession unleash when some one credentialed in another world dares to say anything about activities in the sniper's parish'(p. 39). Methinks he doth protest too much but, at the risk of falling under the same condemnation, we must examine the credentials of this trespasser more carefully!

In reply to the second criticism, Gould made no secret of the fact that he did have a bias, indeed he gloried in it. Furthermore, he claimed that this is true for all of us – that it is impossible for any of us to approach any subject purely objectively. All that can be asked of us is that we treat the subject fairly. With that we can agree, but Gould did much more than merely draw attention to his bias; he embarked on a passionate and eloquent exposition of what he believed. In passing, we are entitled to wonder at what point the weight of scientific evidence would have led him to question, or even abandon, those cherished beliefs, but that would take us too far from our present concerns.

There is one striking aspect of Gould's defence of his factor analysis credentials which does not seem to have attracted criticism and, in anticipation of which, he offered only the most cursory of defences. In brief, Gould was half a century out of date. Factor analysis has moved on since the time he studied it and it is now seen in a different perspective which greatly clarifies the misunderstandings which lie at the root of the 'what is g?' question. The bibliography of the new edition of *The Mismeasure of Man* made no reference at all to any of the extensive literature on factor analysis. In fact there was virtually nothing on any topic published after 1980. In most scientific writing this would be an extraordinary omission. Anyone who professed to teach others medicine or cosmology, for example, on the assumption that no relevant methodology had appeared since the Second World War would not be taken seriously. Gould was not wholly unaware that he had exposed himself to attack from this quarter. He explained why he had not seen fit to update a book that first appeared in 1981 in the following words: '*The Mismeasure of Man* required no update over the first fifteen years because I had focused on the foundation documents of biological determinism, and not on "current" usages so quickly superannuated. I had stressed the deep philosophical errors that do not change rather than the immediate (and superficial) manifestations that become obsolete year by year' (pp. 30–1). This simply will not do so far as factor analysis is concerned. The deep philosophical questions and methods, as they were seen by the founding fathers of factor analysis, have certainly been superannuated, and Gould's understanding with them. To describe the serious research literature in any branch of science as 'superficial manifestations that become obsolete year by year' is, at best, a dangerous and patronising half-truth unworthy of any serious attempt to treat such an important issue.

Principal components analysis is not factor analysis

So what is wrong with Gould's exposition of factor analysis? Are we about to rehearse some of those small-minded cross-border niggles which Gould rightly disdains? After all, Gould seemed rather pleased with his effort, noting in passing, that he had even had complimentary remarks about it from a statistician. Let us not be ungenerous. Gould's account is substantially correct as far as it goes and the ideas were expressed with the clarity and vividness for which the author is renowned. In addition to not getting beyond the first half of the last century, it is not actually about factor analysis at all but about principal components analysis. Up to a point this is not important because, as we have already noted, principal components analysis is a good approximation to factor analysis in many circumstances and, in many respects, it is simpler to explain. In any case Gould is not alone in regarding the two techniques as essentially the same. In fact, many people, including Jensen[4] and Mackintosh,[5] have regarded PCA as just one of several methods of factor analysis and in this they are following a tradition common among psychologists. This view has become enshrined in one of the most popular statistical computer packages, SPSS (Statistics Package for the Social Sciences) where it appears as part of factor analysis. Unfortunately for Gould it is in the difference in the two techniques that the source of his confusion lies.

Gould was, of course, aware of all of this and in the course of a lengthy footnote for aficionados (p. 276) he explains that, though the techniques are different, they 'play the same conceptual role and differ only in mode of calculation'. This puts things the wrong way round. It would be nearer the truth to say that they play a different conceptual role but are similar in mode of calculation. To justify these statements we would have to make an excursion into the modern statistical approach to factor analysis but one point can be made without further ado.

The first principal component extracted from a correlation matrix is a weighted sum of the test scores. At its simplest, these weights might be equal but, usually, different scores will get different weightings. This first component is a score which accounts for as much of the variation among individuals as possible. As explained above, if the test items have been constructed to test intelligence, it is natural to identify this score with what the tests are supposed to be measuring – namely general intelligence. Gould refers to this principal component score as g. But if this were correct, g could not be an intrinsic property of the individual because it clearly depends on which particular test items happen to have been included. Typically, there are many possible test items which could have been included, all with equally good claims to be indicators of basic intelligence. Furthermore, even if the same set of items were administered to the same individual on two occasions, one would hardly expect to get exactly the same score on the second occasion. Each selection will give a different score for a particular individual and, therefore, none can claim to be *the* value of *g*. This may sound like pedantry and will draw the reply that all that is being claimed is that these various components are merely estimating the 'true' *g*. But that is the nub of the matter; we need to find a place for the 'true' *g* within the theory.

How did this situation arise?

Returning to history, Spearman's invention of factor analysis, as we have already noted, was a remarkable achievement. In 1904, when his groundbreaking paper was published, statistical science was in its infancy and multivariate analysis, of which factor analysis is an example, hardly existed. Multivariate analysis, as its name suggests, is concerned with the investigation of the inter-relationships among many variables. Not only was there no adequate conceptual framework within which to formulate such problems, but the heavy computing which the methods required was beyond the reach of the hand calculators of the time. In any case Spearman was a psychologist and any help he might have hoped for from Karl Pearson's Biometrical Laboratory was, apparently, not forthcoming in spite of their proximity in University College London. Despite these handicaps factor analysis did get off the ground and became a flourishing industry driven by the exciting substantive vistas which it opened up.

Principal components analysis did not come on the scene until it was introduced by Hotelling[6] in 1933 although it had been anticipated in a rudimentary form by Karl Pearson around the turn of the century. Interestingly enough, it came to be regarded as a rather superior alternative to factor analysis by most statisticians and that attitude is not uncommon today. This fact may account for the regard in which it also appears to be held by psychologists. Lacking any clear theoretical basis, as judged by the canons of statistics, factor analysis was seen by many as a black art. The development of factor analysis, before the Second World War, was thus largely (but not entirely) left to mathematically minded psychologists. When principal components analysis came along it fitted naturally into the range of methods of doing factor analysis – in effect it is a special case of something known as Principal Axis Factor Analysis[7] which still appears in software packages.

What was lacking was a basis for generalising from the particular circumstances of the test. All IQ tests are carried out on samples of individuals whereas we want to apply the conclusions to some larger population from which they were drawn. Secondly all IQ tests use only a sample of the test items which might have been selected. We really need some basis for claiming that what we infer from any particular battery of tests is much the same as we would have got from any other set of similar items. To approach such questions we need a 'model' which describes how the samples of subjects and items involved in one particular test relate to the wider world to which we want to apply the conclusion. This is what a modern statistical approach to factor analysis provides and this is what was lacking from the older treatment expounded by Gould. It is the most important difference between principal components analysis, which is purely descriptive, and model-based factor analysis which allows us to make inferences. It is the latter which makes it meaningful to speak of 'underlying' factors or 'latent variables' in terms of which g may be defined.

Gould's error

If we have successfully fitted a standard factor model, does that mean that we have proved the existence of a latent variable which we can identify with g? Not quite. What we have done is to demonstrate that what we have observed is what we would have expected to observe if an underlying variable, called g, did exist. It leaves open the possibility that some other mechanism could have produced the observed correlation. To repeat, g is a human construct; that is something which we construct in our minds in order to make sense of what we have observed. For many purposes, it will be legitimate to proceed *as if g* existed and for practical purposes that is often all that matters. There is nothing unusual or scientifically improper in this, it happens all the time. However, the more closely we can link such latent variables to physical structures, like the brain, the better. How far this might be possible in the case of g is something we have already touched on in chapter 5.

Where then did Gould go wrong? First, by failing to distinguish between an empirical index constructed from a set of scores, like a principal component, on the one hand, and an underlying (latent) variable which we can never observe, but about which we can learn something with the aid of a model, on the other. Just what that is, is something we shall come to later, especially in chapter 10. Secondly, by ignoring the fact that we are dealing with samples – of subjects and items – and that this has implications for the inferences we can make.

Gould's treatment of factor analysis also devotes a great deal of attention to something called rotation. It is on the alleged fact that rotation can apparently make factors come and go that Gould bases his most damaging attack. Here too lies another flaw, this time of interpretation, but this is a separate issue which is more conveniently dealt with in the next chapter.

8   One intelligence or many?

The background

One obvious way to take the heat out of much of the debate on intelligence is to recognise that intelligence, as commonly understood, is a complex concept that cannot be captured by a single number. Hardly anyone disputes this. The question is, rather, whether any salient aspect of this many-sided thing can be reduced to numbers, preferably only one.

The attempt to liberate thinking in this field from the seeming straightjacket imposed by the psychometric approach has taken many forms. One has been to identify different sorts of intelligence. So-called 'emotional intelligence'[1] has had a great vogue. This finds its origin in the fact that success in life depends on more than the skills tested by conventional IQ tests. 'Spiritual intelligence'[2] has been floated though, so far, without quite the same appeal. The advocates of such 'new' intelligences often seem to successfully convey the idea that theirs is subtly superior to the more mundane version. There may well, of course, be good reasons for introducing new measures of human characteristics on these lines. If there are, they will need to be explored with the same rigour and thoroughness as has been devoted to the mental ability which is the subject of this book. If this happens, it is highly likely the new indices will encounter precisely the same problems and criticisms. In particular, that the notion is a complex one which cannot be adequately condensed into a single number! One of the best known advocates of this broader approach to intelligence is Howard Gardner[3] who has developed a theory of what he calls *multiple intelligences*. We shall return to his ideas later in the chapter.

Sternberg[4] is another leader in the field who has argued for a broader view of intelligence. He has proposed a triarchic theory in which the first branch is Analytic Intelligence, the second is Practical Intelligence and the third is Creative Intelligence. Of these, analytical intelligence comes closest to g.

There is a pragmatic answer to the question of the chapter title which seems to have been adopted, almost by default, by those in the empirical IQ tradition. It is, essentially, that whatever other aspects of intelligence there may be, IQ is useful. In particular, that it is useful for predicting future success in tasks requiring 'intelligence'. This is precisely the way it was used in the US armed forces in two world wars and for testing adults applying for their first job. There is no doubt that these tests influenced the lives of millions of individuals and that there was widespread agreement that the exercise was worthwhile.

The situation today is rather different. The focus has moved to what psycho-metric tests tell us about the nature of the human person. This has immense implications for the way that society is ordered. In so far as the results of testing claim to provide a scientific basis for political programmes, their effects go much further and deeper. The perception, in some quarters, that an individual's worth can be summed up in a single number, effectively fixed at birth, has become a potent symbol of the danger to society of giving credence to what many see as pseudo-science. Although the effects are less direct, they are more profound than they were when tests were used primarily for selection. It is, therefore, important to examine the scientific status of the claims and counter-claims very carefully. Nowhere is this more necessary than in the matter of multiple intelligences.

Thurstone's multiple factor idea

Life would have been much simpler if Spearman's hypothesis of a single dimen-sion of ability had turned out to be true. In particular, testing ability would have been a relatively simple matter. Any collection of tests depending on mental ability would have revealed the same underlying factor. The mysterious quan-tity g, whose nature we are trying to elucidate, would then be identified with the common source of variation which underlies all these tests. However, as we reported in chapter 2, things turned out otherwise as it became clear that varia-tion in one dimension was not sufficient to explain individual differences in test performance. In the language of chapter 6, it simply was not possible to find any single sufficient statistic which fully accounted for the correlations. This simple empirical fact underlies much of the fiercest current debate on whether g exists and, if so, what it is. In this chapter we shall aim to clarify what it means when individual ability varies in more than one dimension and aim to show whether the notion of g can survive this new complication.

The simplicity of Spearman's idea of a single underlying factor was gradually eroded and Thorndike[5] and Thurstone's multiple factor idea became a serious rival. According to both of them there was not a single general ability but several, which Thurstone called primary abilities. He showed that the pattern of correlations among test scores supported the hypothesis that these test items fell into groups, each corresponding to one of his primary abilities. To make the point very simply, suppose that the battery of tests contains items directed to numeracy and literacy. The former requires ability with numbers, the latter ability with words. Numeracy and literacy might therefore be examples of primary abilities which, it could be argued, were more fundamental than a single 'general' ability. Furthermore, it could also be argued that they were more useful, since, in selecting children for careers, it would be more relevant to identify whether their particular mix of numerical and verbal abilities was right for the job in view. Thurstone, in fact, identified more than two primary abilities[6] but the point at issue is most simply made by reference to two. At a stroke, therefore, Thurstone appeared to have demolished the notion of g and replaced it with something which seemed both more realistic and more useful.

A hierarchy of factors?

Nevertheless, as we explained in chapter 2, Spearman's battle was not lost and the idea of a single general factor made a comeback. There we noted that Thurstone's primary abilities were themselves correlated. Thus, in our hypothetical example, individuals who were high on the numeracy scale would also tend to be high on literacy. Given a set of primary abilities, all positively correlated among themselves, it was possible to argue about them in precisely the same way as about the original test items. Thus g re-emerged as the general factor underlying all test performance but now it appeared to be even more fundamental. Since Thurstone's day this idea has sometimes been elaborated to include several levels of factors but, at the deepest level, researchers have claimed to find a single common factor which might be identified with g. This hierarchical view of the matter is held by many of the leading protagonists on the psychometric side of the great g debate.[7] We shall see later that this development of factor analysis is not necessary though, in some ways, it can be illuminating.[8]

The gist of the arguments put forward by the advocates of a fundamental underlying factor is, therefore, that however you factor analyse the results of test scores there is no way of banishing g. Always, at the deepest level, there emerges this fundamental quantity. The identification of primary abilities did not abolish g, they argue, but merely gave it a more fundamental role. In order to evaluate these arguments we shall have to examine carefully what it means to say that individual variation is multidimensional. To do this we shall move outside the field of testing altogether and construct an analogy which may help to make the matter clear, without the ideological baggage which be-devils so much contemporary discussion of the issues.

Variation in two dimensions

Let us consider the location of cities on a map, more specifically, the map of England. No one doubts that cities vary in their location! Describing that variation is necessary for constructing a mental picture of where one city is in relation to another and for providing travel instructions to get from one to the other. If England were a linear entity, like a motorway, it would be a simple matter to describe the position of cities by their distance from one end. Variation in location would then be one-dimensional and could be expressed on some scale of distance. It would suffice to say that two cities were 45 miles apart, for example. But the geography of England is not one-dimensional. To a good approximation it is two-dimensional as it appears on road maps. We cannot then describe the location of a place in terms of a single figure – distance – but we need two figures. There is an unlimited number of ways in which we can do this and the choice of one over another is arbitrary.

Consider, for example the cities of London and Manchester. We can describe where Manchester is in relation to London in the form of instructions we might give to a London helicopter pilot free to fly in any direction at will. We could say 'go so many miles north, turn left at right angles, and then go so many miles west'. Alternatively we could say 'fly so many miles north-west, turn right and fly so many miles north-east'. Either way the pilot would end up in Manchester, although the directions and flight path would have been different in each case. Another alternative would be to give a bearing on which the pilot should fly out of London expressed as an angle between the flight path and some fixed direction, like magnetic north, and then to say how many miles had to be flown on that bearing. However the instructions are given, we need two numbers, either two distances or one angle and one distance. There is nothing fictitious about London and Manchester and there is no question that they are not in the same place! When we come to describe their position relative to one another, however, there is an arbitrariness in how we do it. One or other method may be better *for some purpose* but neither is superior in any absolute sense.

To put the matter in other, and slightly more sophisticated geographical terms, we can locate any point on the map by its longitude and its latitude. On the surface of the globe we measure longitude and latitude by degrees because we are referring to distances along the arc of a circle. For relatively small areas, like the map of England, the curvature can be ignored and latitude and longitude provide a rectangular grid with the aid of which we can locate points on the map. From that we can plot a route from one point to another, measure the distance between them and so on.

If we couch the discussion in terms of where people reside, we can say that the locations of their residences vary and that it needs two dimensions to describe that variation fully. We find ourselves in exactly the same position with factor analysis where, at least, two latent dimensions prove to be necessary to describe the mutual correlations. If two dimensions suffice, a two-dimensional space is then needed to describe the positions of individuals and those positions are defined by the equivalent of map references. To summarise: location on a geographical map is two-dimensional. This should prepare us for the idea that intelligence may also be a two- or, perhaps, a many-dimensional entity.

The convention of using latitude and longitude to define the position of points on a map is so deeply ingrained that it is difficult to imagine using any other reference grid but, as we have noted in relation to London and Manchester, there is no reason, in principle, why this should not be done. There may be no reason to wonder why we use longitude and latitude but, in the factor analysis context, where there is no natural grid, we have to consider how to choose among the various options.

Variation in more dimensions: a dominant dimension

Thinking about simple geographical analogies should not lead us to overlook the fact that there may need to be more than two dimensions. We can get some inkling of what is involved when moving to three dimensions by thinking of a country like Chile. Chile is a long thin country, running roughly north and south, which includes part of the Andean mountain range. It is about 2650 miles from north to south, about 110 miles wide from east to west and roughly four miles high at its highest point. Location is thus a three-dimensional entity and an accurate determination of location therefore requires three numbers: longitude, latitude and altitude.

However, quite a good idea of the location of a place in Chile can be conveyed by just two numbers, the longitude and latitude. This is because the variation in altitude is much less than in the case of the other two dimensions. Little more is lost by discarding the longitude, which also varies relatively little, and relying solely on the latitude – or, what comes to much the same thing – the number of miles from the southern tip of Chile. If we were to draw a line running from north to south up the centre of the country, and were to regard the position of all locations as being on this line at the appropriate number of miles from the southernmost point, we would never be much more than about fifty miles out. The latitude is thus the *dominant dimension* in this case.

The fact that Chile runs roughly north and south made it much easier to see that location in that country could be approximately specified by a single number. Moving on to two dimensions, latitude and longitude were ready-made dimensions to which a location could be related. If Chile had been the same shape, but with its major axis running from north-east to south-west, latitude alone would have not been enough. We would still have needed latitude and longitude to get a good fix. However, a glance at the map would have shown us that a line drawn up the middle of the country from south-west to north-east would have done the trick of reducing the number of dimensions needed to one.

Before returning to intelligence it is worth adding a further illustration to underline the point that the identification of a dominant dimension has nothing to do with geography. The location of a person on a passenger aircraft is described by two numbers – the row number and the seat number (in practice, usually a letter). Of these the row number is the most important if we want to find someone. For this purpose, the length dimension of the aircraft dominates the width.

Intelligence, as that term is commonly used, is also a many-dimensional entity. This fact is revealed by factor analysis. The main IQ tests, such as the Wechsler Adult Intelligence Scale (WAIS), consist of many items. When the test scores are subjected to factor analysis, it turns out that several dimensions are needed to give a reasonable fit to the data. The 'intelligence' measured by that scale is, therefore, not the one-dimensional thing that many of its critics have supposed it to be. Wechsler, for his part, never claimed that it was. On the contrary, the scale was explicitly constructed to capture several distinct aspects of intelligence. Thus there were groups of items on Information, Comprehension, Arithmetical Reasoning, Memory Span for Digits, Similarities, Picture Arrangement, Picture Completion, Block Design, Digit Symbol, Object Assembly and Vocabulary. Although this scale was not designed within a factor analysis framework, it subsequently turned out that about three dimensions were sufficient to describe most of the variation. Of those three dimensions, one was dominant in much the same way as latitude proved to be in the example of Chile. It was this dominant dimension that was subsequently recognised as g.

In view of the persistent claims that psychometricians have regarded intelligence as a unitary one-dimensional entity, it is worth quoting Matarazzo (in his revision of Wechsler's *The Measurement of Adult Intelligence*): '. . . a person's general or overall intelligence as reflected in Binet's early index or in a modern IQ score is not a measure of a single unitary entity but, rather, a complex index of interacting variables which are expressed by this single, final, or common index (the IQ score)' (p. 261).

When investigating the dimensionality of intelligence, there are no ready-made directions, such as latitude and longitude provide, to enable us to 'get our bearings'. We have to start from scratch looking for the direction of greatest variation. The search can be broken down into two stages. First we need a means of measuring the relative importance of any set of dimensions and thus of finding the one which is dominant for that set. Then we have to compare all possible choices to see which yields the 'most dominant' dimension. In the Chile example the first step was easy; all distances were measured in miles and it was merely a matter of picking out the largest of three distances. The second step would have been to consider all the ways we could have positioned the axes and then to choose the one which yielded the maximum dominant dimension.

Finding the dominant dimension

The geographical analogy appears to let us down when we try to identify the dominant dimension in factor analysis. The dominant dimension, we recall is the one having the highest degree of variation. In principal components analysis, the problem does not arise because the whole method is set up to produce an index with the greatest variation. However, in factor analysis, we have been at pains to emphasise that we can learn nothing about the scale or the origin of the factors. How, then, can we discover the one with the greatest variation if we cannot measure variation? We must digress, briefly, to elucidate the answer to this question.

Although we cannot determine the variance, say, of any factor, we can find something which is almost as good. We start with what is called the *total variation* of the indicators. It is then possible to break this down into parts, each of which can be linked to one of the factors, together with one left over to cover the residual variation not arising from the factors. This enables us to say how much each factor contributes to the total variation and, therefore, determines the *relative* importance of each factor.[9] The dominant factor is the one which makes the greatest contribution. If, for example, the dominant factor accounted for something like 50 per cent of the variation with the rest being shared between three or four other factors and the residual, we might feel that the analysis had uncovered a dominant factor of some significance. This is roughly the position we find ourselves in when analysing data from intelligence tests.

All of this pre-supposes that we have decided which is the appropriate grid reference system to use for the factor space. With no ready-made 'latitude' and 'longitude' we have to search for the 'directions', such that the dominant dimension has the largest possible relative variation. The technical term for this search exercise is *rotation*.

Rotation

The arbitrariness of the way in which the position of points in a plane are defined, lies at the root of much criticism of factor analysis as a tool for studying human abilities. If we identify *g* with one particular dimension then, if we change to another grid reference system, that dimension no longer figures in our description of the location of a particular point. How can anything be described as real which vanishes as we move from one system of reference to another? This is at the heart of Gould's dismissal of factor analysis as a tool for studying intelligence and, implicitly, that of Rose also.

The process of selecting other systems of reference in factor analysis is known as *rotation*. To picture this let us go back to the map of England and then imagine that the grid reference system is pivoted on the meridian line at Greenwich, say. We can then think of the whole system being rotated about that point so that the lines of longitude, which originally ran north and south, now move through an angle until, say, they lie in a north-west to south-east direction. We can define the position of any point on the map by reference to the rotated system and this, in principle, would serve equally well. Does any particular rotational switch have special claims to our attention? We can best approach this question by continuing with the analogy of the map.

There are two grounds on which a particular rotation might have claims to be considered significant, one empirical on the lines described above and one substantive. Starting with the empirical, we look at the importance of the contribution which any particular dimension makes to the total description of any point's location. This was the situation in our discussion of the geography of Chile, where the single north–south dimension was much the most important. Let us take this idea a little further in relation to the map of England. Suppose we had to make do with only one figure to specify the location of a point on a two-dimensional map of England. Because England is relatively long and thin in a north–south direction, latitude has a particular claim on our attention. Manchester could be described as so many miles or degrees north of London and though this would not take us precisely to Manchester it would get us nearer than many other rotations. Of course the rotation which goes directly through Manchester would enable us to specify Manchester's position exactly by only one number, but the same reference system would not work so well for Hull, Leeds or Southampton. The best general purpose system for all cities relying on one dimension only would probably be something close to the north–south axis. One way of describing why we might choose to use this direction is to say that the variation (scatter) between cities is greater in this direction than in any other. Similarly, when we have any two-dimensional factor, we can ask what rotation will be such that one of the axes corresponds to the direction of greatest variation. In an obvious sense this is the most important direction, because it gives us more information than any other single direction about the location of the city in which we are interested. If g is to be regarded as *the* fundamental latent variable then we would expect to find it emerging as the axis with greatest variation between individuals.

A second, substantive, way of choosing an optimal rotation is by relating the axes to some relevant physical characteristic. If, for example, we were interested in the likely success of growing grape vines in England, where temperature is an important factor for the ripening process, we might note that mean temperature falls off as we go from south to north. The north–south axis, or latitude, therefore corresponds to a physical property of the solar system which, in the northern hemisphere, leads to higher temperatures, on average, in the south than in the north. On the other hand, if it was rainfall that was crucial, the east–west dimension would be more important in a country like England. Yet again, if it was the combination of rainfall and temperature that mattered most, an axis joining London to the north-west or south-west might be the most relevant direction. In the factor analysis of test scores the analogy is to consider whether the axes of a particular rotation correspond in some way to physical attributes of the person or, more particularly, the person's brain. The purpose of rotation is then to find the most *relevant* description of the latent space for the particular purpose in mind.[10]

Does rotation dispose of g?

We are now in a position to answer the criticism of Gould, Rose and others that g cannot be real because it can be 'rotated away'. What the analysis of test scores actually establishes is that people vary in their performance on mental tests and that it takes more than one dimension to describe fully that variation. Just as Manchester is not located in the same place as London, so Jane differs from Thomas in ability. The variation is *real*: the means of describing it is arbitrary but not meaningless. To go back to an earlier example, there is a choice as to whether we choose to describe that difference in terms of arithmetical and verbal primary abilities, say, or in terms of general ability and a bi-polar dimension distinguishing the numerate from the literate. It is not the case that one way is right and the other wrong, it is simply that they are different but *equivalent*. They are as real as the variation which they describe.

Nevertheless, one may feel that this argument is damaging to the notion of g because, at best, it now appears as only one among several possible ways of describing the variation. Is there anything to give it primacy? The only empirical criterion that is available is the one of relative importance or dominance. Imagine that we choose that rotation which makes g one of the axes and then ask which dimension we would keep if we were compelled to throw all but one away. In the example of defining the position of Manchester in relation to London, we recognised that the north–south axis would be of most use because it would get us nearer than most others. Or, put another way, the major direction of variation in distance in the UK is in the north–south direction. Substantively, one might add that the north–south dimension is deeply embedded in the public mind because of its cultural and climatic connotations. Similarly, g's claim to priority must rest, first, on the fact (if, indeed, it turns out to be a fact) that individuals show more variation on that dimension than any other and secondly that it corresponds closely to what we understand by 'general intelligence'.

Our answer to the question of the chapter title is thus that it is not an either/or matter at all. It is that intelligence is a many dimensional entity. However, it is worth asking whether there is a dominant dimension which is both useful and meaningful. The discovery of such a single dimension, called g, is the result of that search.

Frames of mind

This is the title of Howard Gardner's book[11] in which he sets out an alternative approach to intelligence which, in essence, answers the question of the chapter title by saying that there are many intelligences.

Gardner's work in this area is a major contribution to the study of intelligence which some have regarded as an alternative to the psychometric approach. Gardner himself does not take such a hard line, though he does believe that there are important differences between the two approaches. His use of the word intelligences, in the plural, is deliberate though critics have suggested that 'abilities' or 'skills' would be a more appropriate word. His principal criticism of the psychometric approach is that it is not rooted in the biology of the brain, but is a purely mathematical summarisation of correlations. Gardner aims to root his theory in the brain, which is obviously the basis of intelligence whatever that should turn out to be. He notes that there are quite distinct abilities, like musical ability, which seem to be associated with a particular part of the brain. This becomes clear when part of the brain is damaged and yet certain specific abilities appear to be unimpaired. Conversely, damage to a particular part of the brain may effectively remove some particular ability without affecting other abilities. This identification of areas of the brain with particular functions provides a biological basis for postulating the existence of multiple intelligences.

There are clearly some similarities between Gardner's multiple intelligences and Thurstone's version of the multiple factor view of intelligence. Both, for example, identify about seven specific abilities or intelligences but Gardner points out that, whereas Thurstone's factors are purely mathematical artefacts, his intelligences have a physical basis in the brain.

Jensen, however, has pointed out that some of Gardner's intelligences correspond to the dimensions of ability that have been revealed by the psychometric approach. This may be seen as providing biological backing for factors uncovered by purely statistical methods. Jensen further observes that Gardner's special intelligences are only exhibited by people with relatively high IQs, greater than about 120, who constitute a very small proportion of the population.[12] It is unclear whether or not a broader psychometric investigation would reveal new dimensions, corresponding to Gardner's other intelligences. Jensen, among others, sees Gardner's theory as a purely descriptive account, which has some points of contact with psychometric theory but does not contradict it. However, Gardner's way of looking at intelligence is illuminating, especially in drawing attention to a possible biological basis for dimensions (factors) discovered statistically, but it does not undermine the basic framework within which we are operating.

There have been other ways of describing the factor space, some very elaborate. One of the best known is due to Cattell[13] who introduced *crystallised intelligence* (G_c) and *fluid intelligence* (G_f). To these were added various 'second order factors', each identified by a subscript (G_v, G_r, G_s, etc.). The record in this sphere must go to Guilford whose 'structure of intellect' study claimed to have found upwards of ninety factors (the precise number depends on how they are enumerated and classified).[14] From a statistical point of view, one thing can be confidently asserted. Factor analysis is incapable of identifying more than a handful of factors, with any precision, unless the sample size is very large indeed. Claims to have done otherwise can, therefore, be taken with a large pinch of the proverbial salt. The existence of other ways of describing the factor space does not undermine the account we have given focusing on *g*. They merely illustrate, again, that there are many equivalent ways of describing a multidimensional thing like intelligence. The question is: which is the more relevant or useful for a particular purpose? On these pragmatic grounds, we can say that there are many circumstances in which it is advantageous to use the one in which *g* is the dominant dimension.

9   The Bell Curve: facts, fallacies and speculations

Status of the Curve

We have been rather dismissive of the Bell Curve. It would be fair to summarise our position so far as being that the Bell Curve plays no fundamental part in the measurement of intelligence. The reasons for the central role accorded it by Herrnstein and Murray were never adequately spelt out but they do seem to have recognised that it was an artefact.[1] We have argued that, as a description of the distribution of g, it is pure fiction; a useful fiction perhaps, but a fiction nonetheless. Perhaps the situation is not unlike that said to obtain between mathematicians and physicists. Mathematicians worked on the Bell Curve because they believed the physicists had shown it to be an empirical fact, whereas physicists used it because they thought the mathematicians had proved a theorem which required its use!

Unlike g, IQ is an empirical index so it certainly has an observable distribution in any population. Furthermore there are good reasons, which we shall enumerate below, for expecting the distribution to be rather like the Bell Curve. Nevertheless, Wechsler, for example, understood that anything purporting to measure intelligence must necessarily have an arbitrary distribution and hence that he was at liberty to choose anything that was convenient. He, therefore, decided to calibrate his measures in such a way as to make their distribution conform precisely to the Bell Curve.[2] The use of this curve was, therefore, no more than a convention, not an empirical fact at all.

But perhaps, we have been a little too hasty in dismissing the Bell Curve in such uncompromising terms. This particular distribution is deeply rooted in statistics and was surely not adopted by the IQ community without the feeling that there was some benefit in so doing, so let us take a step back and look at this curve afresh.[3] First, we give some basic facts about the distribution and point out the bearing they have on intelligence testing. Then we move into more speculative mode with the intention of gaining more insight into why g and IQ vary, and whether there might be any grounds for treating their distributions as conforming to the Bell Curve.

What is the Bell Curve?

To begin with the name; the term 'the Bell Curve', in this context, appears to be an invention of Murray and Herrnstein intended, no doubt, to take advantage of the memorable bell-like shape of the frequency curve. In this they were following generations of teachers who have defined this distribution and then, in order to fix its shape in the minds of students, have described it as bell-shaped. In ordinary statistical discourse it is most commonly called the *normal* distribution, or sometimes, the *Gaussian* distribution after Gauss the celebrated mathematician. Normal is an unfortunate term because it seems to imply that any other distribution is, in some sense, abnormal. There may have been a time when this did, indeed, appear to be the case. The origins of the Curve lie in the theory of errors where it was believed to describe the distribution of errors made in making repeated observations on, for example, some astronomical quantity. It was in that connection that Gauss comes into the story. However, by the turn of the nineteenth century it was becoming clear that many distributions did not have this shape and the early statisticians and biometricians began to study families of distributions embracing a much wider variety of shapes. We shall usually prefer the name 'normal' here because it enables us to say that something is 'normally distributed' or, is normal, whereas the necessary part of speech is lacking if we speak of the Bell Curve.

Figure 9.1 shows the Bell Curve. Because of the symmetry, the average lies at the centre, as does the median – the point above and below which half the distribution lies. The range is unrestricted which in theory means that there is no limit on how extreme an observation can be. There is not one Bell Curve but many and they differ from one another in location and dispersion. Figure 9.2 shows two curves which have different locations but the same dispersion. The members of the top distribution tend to have smaller values than those in the bottom distribution. In other words the former are located lower on the scale which is assumed to increase from left to right. Figure 9.3 shows two distributions which differ in dispersion, but have the same location. The members

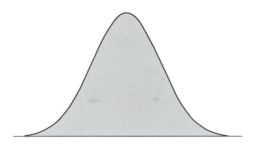

Figure 9.1 The normal distribution or 'Bell Curve'.

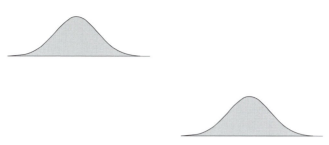

Figure 9.2 Two normal distributions with different locations.

of the dotted distribution are more spread out than those in the solid distribution. It is important to be able to recognise these distinctions when inspecting distributions. Often, of course, distributions will differ in both location and spread.

The spread of a distribution is often measured by what is called the standard deviation. We do not need to know how this is calculated, but it is useful to remember that half of the distribution is contained within a distance of two-thirds of a standard deviation of the average, and that an interval of two standard deviations on either side of the average includes 95 per cent of the distribution. These two numbers, the average and the standard deviation, determine the distribution completely. This means that if we have these two quantities we can construct the whole distribution. Conversely, any difference between two normal distributions can be specified in terms of one or both of these numbers. This is an extremely useful fact.

Why is the Bell Curve so important?

There are three inter-related reasons why the normal distribution is so central in statistics. These will enable us to see why it seems so natural to bring it into the measurement of intelligence.

First, as we have just noted, there are many quantities in nature which turn out to have a distribution which is either normal or close to normal. For example, apart from error distributions, many biological measurements such as height, length or weight of plants or parts of individuals turn out to have distributions of roughly this form. None of these will be exactly normal, as one can easily see by observing that the normal distribution has an unlimited range in both directions, whereas lengths and weights are necessarily positive. Nevertheless, to a good approximation, examples of the Bell Curve are common in the study of biological variation. Similarly there are many quantities in the social sciences which have such a distribution of which sums of test scores are a good example.

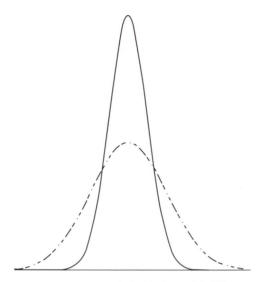

Figure 9.3 Two normal distributions with different spreads.

There is some empirical justification for the convention that IQ, as originally defined, be treated as normal. We saw, in chapter 2, that the earliest definition was based on mental age and that IQ defined in this way turned out to be approximately normal. However we also noted that this was not a satisfactory definition, even for children, because it did not remain fixed throughout childhood. Nevertheless, it was close enough to later and better definitions to expect them to be approximately normal also – as, indeed, they turned out to be. For reasons which will become clear in a moment, total scores obtained by adding up individual marks of any kind tend to have normal distributions.

Secondly, in the theory of statistics, we often need to make assumptions about distributions which we cannot observe directly. The normal distribution is a particularly convenient assumption to make because it has many attractive mathematical properties which makes the analysis and development of new methods that much easier. This might seem to be a very unsatisfactory reason for making an assumption, because correspondence to the truth is surely more important than mathematical or any other kind of convenience. This is true, but even if the distribution of the quantity in which we are interested is not normal we can often make it is so by an appropriate transformation (re-scaling). In effect, we are then re-phrasing the question so that it can be answered within the capabilities of existing methods. There is no need to go into the details of what this means except to remark that the questions which we ask of the data can often just as easily be answered by considering, say, the logarithm or square root of the variable rather than the variable itself. If one or other of these has a distribution which is closer to the normal, then we would obviously prefer the analysis based on that transformation in order to take advantage of the normal distribution's attractive properties. We can then, as it were, take a method 'off the shelf' rather than have to develop something new. There might be good reasons for re-phrasing the questions we ask in intelligence testing so that they can be answered within the familiar ambit of the Bell Curve.

The third, and most important reason, why the normal distribution has such a central role, is that its occurrence is predictable on theoretical grounds in certain very common situations. This depends upon a famous theorem in probability theory known as the *Central Limit Theorem*.[4] In its simplest form this is concerned with the distribution of sums of component variables which are independent of one another and have the same distribution. Suppose, for example, that the marks awarded by an examiner to a sample of answers on a particular question in an examination vary, but that the pattern of variation (it does not have to be normal and usually will not be) is the same on all questions on a particular paper. Then the Central Limit Theorem says that, if the number of items is large enough, the distribution of the sum will be approximately normal. In practice this is often a very good approximation even when adding up as few as four or five individual marks. Sums and averages arise very commonly in many applied contexts and the Central Limit Theorem then assures us that, without knowing the individual distributions of the component items, the distribution of the sum will be approximately normal.

For the argument which we shall make in a moment, we shall need a rather more general form of the Central Limit Theorem covering two additional features. The first concerns what happens if the components of the sum have different distributions. It turns out that the distribution will still be approximately normal, providing that a rather important condition is satisfied. We do not need to specify this mathematically but the essence is that the contribution of each item to the sum shall be relatively small, with no individual item having too dominant a role. If one particular item was subject to very much greater variability than any of the others, its effect would not to be sufficiently diluted by the cumulative effect of the others and then the normality would be undermined. The second feature concerns possible correlations between the variables. Again, we do not need to go into the technical details but provided that the correlations are not too large, and that the number of items is large enough, there will still be a tendency for the normal distribution to arise. What applies to simple sums also applies to weighted sums, so many of the commonest measures are covered in one way or another. Roughly speaking we are saying that a sum (or average or weighted sum) will be approximately normal if it is made up of a largish number of components, if none of them is dominant and if each adds something not included in the other contributions.

We now have to consider whether any or all of these considerations are relevant to the distribution of indices of intelligence like IQ or latent variables like g.

Why might IQ or g be treated as normal?

In this, and the following section, we move more explicitly into speculative mode. However, this is speculation with a purpose. Even if any choice of distribution for IQ or g is only a matter of convention, such conventions have to be established and it is desirable that they be rationally based. We therefore have to consider whether there are good reasons for the universal practice of making IQ conform to a normal distribution. Similarly, we need to know whether there are good reasons for treating g as normal in those circumstances where such an assumption is needed.

In the case of IQ the answer is relatively easy. Most IQ test scores are arrived at by adding up the answers provided by subjects to a fairly large set of test items. Given that these items are all designed to tap the same underlying dimension of ability, the responses will not be independent – if they were the test would be useless – but there will still be a tendency to normality ensured by the more general versions of the Central Limit Theorem. There is thus a good theoretical reason for believing we shall not have to do too much violence to the empirical distribution to transform it to normality as Wechsler's convention requires.

The case of g is much trickier. Because we can never observe it directly, we can never observe its distribution. We have already shown, in chapter 6, that the distribution of any sufficient statistic, designed to capture all that the data have to tell us about g, is not unique. In chapter 10, we shall return to the question and show that there are theoretical arguments which show that there is no way of even estimating the distribution without making un-testable assumptions. If we are to get any idea of what would be a suitable convention for the distribution of g, it will have to be deduced from any insight we can gain into how g is related to what goes on in the brain or, perhaps, by finding parallels with other phenomena. For this to be possible, g has to be more than a purely constructed entity having no physical basis. It would be absurd to suppose that lurking somewhere within the brain is some kind of physical entity to which we can take a measuring instrument and come away with a value of g. If g has a basis in the physical structure or function of the brain, it must be as some kind of collective measure of relevant brain characteristics. This takes us back to our earlier description of g as a dual measure in chapter 5.

The brain is a highly complex system involving a vast numbers of synapses and complicated interactions between its different parts. One can imagine monitoring brain processes with a series of instruments, each one designed to record some aspect of brain activity. We might then imagine that we have to construct a summary measure which reflects the overall power or performance of the brain. If we were to do this by factor analysis, and were to find a dominant factor, it would be tempting to identify this with the g to which we had been led by analysing the outputs of the brain recorded in the answers to test items. If we were able to estimate it, we could ask whether it was highly correlated with the g-score, say. If so, we could plausibly regard it as the basis of g.

There is an analogy here with the way in which we construct an index of IQ which aims to summarise a relevant collective property of a series of tests. We are now speculating that g can be regarded, similarly, as a collective property of a large number of physical attributes of the brain. As such it would not, of course, convey all there is to be said about the performance of the brain, but we might hope that it would capture the principal dimension of brain performance which would be indirectly observed via the kind of items which form part of intelligence tests. What then are the physical properties of the brain that we might plausibly regard as indicative of general intelligence?

Attempts have been made to identify brain characteristics which might correspond to g as we have described it.[5] One of the simplest and crudest of such measures is brain volume. The brain has a very convoluted shape and it is not easy to measure its volume. Gould and others have lampooned earlier attempts to measure volume posthumously, for example, by filling skulls with lead shot. However, it is now possible to do this accurately using magnetic resonance scanners. Maybe larger brains have more functionality and hence give their owners better intellectual performance. This cannot be true in general because men on average have larger brains than women but display no significant advantage in cognitive performance. Within the sexes, however, a modest correlation has been observed between brain size and IQ of the order of 0.4. Gould repeatedly claimed that there was no such correlation, but such a claim can now only be maintained if one ignores a substantial research literature on the subject.[6] Because of the lack of a sex difference, it has been speculated that it is not size as such but the number of neural connections or something similar within the brain which matters; maybe they are more closely packed in women than in men. Our purpose here is not to build a brain-based theory of g but, more modestly, to indicate the direction in which one might look. Other quantities that seem relevant have to do with the speed with which the brain processes information. There is a substantial current research effort on measuring response times in simple situations and it appears that measured speed does correlate positively with scores on IQ tests.[7] There is at least a reasonable prospect that, as research progresses in this direction, it will be possible to provide g with a physical basis.

Of itself, this does not obviously take us any nearer a basis for treating g as normal. But it does make g rather more like size and shape which, as we saw, are collective properties of measurements made on physical objects. If g were a collective property of physical attributes of the brain, it might be that some common ground could be found with these other collective properties for which we feel on surer ground when talking about their distributions.

One reasonable starting point is to look at other normally distributed quantities where we do have some idea of why they have that distribution. From what we have already said about the central limit theorem, we might start by looking for quantities which can be regarded as sums of a large number of contributions.

Let us look again at the question of the height of the human person which we have already considered in another context. This varies considerably between individuals and we know that its distribution is very approximately normal. There are few very tall people and few very short people with the great majority falling somewhere in between. The explanation of the normality of height, as of many other biological measures, is usually traced back to the genetics of inheritance. If there were a single gene for height we might expect its inheritance to be a relatively simpler matter. The offspring's height would most likely be somewhere close to that of the two parents. However, height is something which is affected by many genes and also by a great many environmental factors and so the relationship will be much less clear cut. If each of many genes makes a small contribution to the final height, as do the many and varying circumstances of nutrition and upbringing, then we have a situation which is reminiscent of the conditions required for the central limit theorem. We should not therefore be surprised to find that height is indeed approximately normally distributed because it is determined by a very large number of factors, each of which would only have a small effect by itself.

If similar considerations apply to the constituent parts of the brain, then each of those which bear upon mental performance might be expected to be roughly normal. Consequently any collective property measured by an average of the constituent contributions would also be close to normal in the form of its distribution. Thus, although there is no way in which we can determine the distribution of g from the data provided by intelligence tests, it is reasonable, but no more, to treat it as if it had a normal distribution. The conventional scaling, assuming normality, thus has, perhaps, a little more substance than do many of the alternatives.

The assumptions required by the Central Limit Theorem sounded innocent enough so it may come, initially, as a surprise to the reader that one, at least, is often false. Furthermore, this happens in common and important circumstances. Normality required that no individual determinant should play a dominant role. In the case of height, and many other things, the presence or absence of a Y chromosome makes a great deal of difference. The average difference in height between males and females is several inches. Thus although we may apply the central limit argument to men or women separately, it does not work if they are treated as a single population. What we get then is a mixture of two Bell Curves. Figure 9.4 illustrates the position.

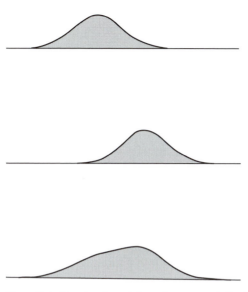

Figure 9.4 Showing the mixing of two normal distributions.

The upper and middle parts of the diagram show two normal distributions with different averages. The lower part shows what happens when they are merged. The resulting distribution is clearly not bell-shaped. This simple example makes a very important point about what it might be reasonable to assume about the shape of distributions. If there are two (or several) sub-groups in a population, each having different normal distributions, then the distribution of the combined groups cannot also be normal – and conversely. This applies whether the difference between the components is in the average, as in this example, or in the dispersion. When we come to consider possible differences between ethnic groups in chapter 11 the answers we get will depend on how we define the populations involved.

The position rapidly becomes more complicated if there are several ways of forming sub-groups. The heterogeneity introduced makes it more difficult to see what the resulting mixture will look like. Nevertheless it remains true that one cannot have it both ways; if the component distributions are different Bell Curves, the mixture will not be.[8]

Intuitions on the spacing of individuals

There is one further point to be made and, even though it is subjective and imprecise, it does appear to weigh quite heavily with many who come fresh to this topic. This is that many people appear to have some feeling for the kind of

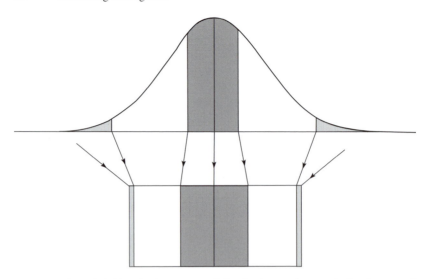

Figure 9.5 Showing how a normal distribution can be stretched and squeezed to make it rectangular.

spacing which *ought* to arise when people are distributed along a scale according to their intelligence. This may be expressed by saying that they feel that the majority are close to average, and are not readily distinguishable, whereas, at the extremes, there are fewer people and those few are more spread out. It is hard to know whether this is a reading back into the data of something which the Bell Curve leads us to expect, or whether it is a more empirically based insight which, though real enough, is hard to pin down.

The point can be made more clearly, perhaps, by pursuing the implications of our earlier statement that the form of the distribution of *g* is largely arbitrary. We have just been making a case for treating it as normal but we could perfectly well give it any other form. For example, we could make it rectangular. A rectangular distribution takes its name from its shape which, instead of appearing like a bell, is now a rectangle. To transform a normal distribution into a rectangular distribution, we would have to squeeze up the tails of the normal so that more individuals were packed into shorter intervals, and we would have to spread out the centre of the distribution and go on doing this until equal intervals on the new measurement scale contained equal numbers of individuals. In figure 9.5 we have illustrated this transformation by showing how intervals containing equal amounts of probability match up. To make things clearer, the rectangular distribution is printed upside down so that the base of one distribution projects onto the base of the other.[9]

We can conventionally label the new scale as extending from zero at the left-hand end to one at the right-hand end. This method of scaling individuals has some attractive properties. For example, if we are told that an individual's scale value is 0.54, that tells us immediately that 54 per cent of the population lie below that individual on the scale and 46 per cent above him. In other words, an individual's scale value is also their 'percentile'.

People tend to feel uneasy with this new scaling because it packs individuals in as densely at the extremes as in the middle and this does not seem to be the way things are. Teachers, especially in mathematics, know that there are large differences in mathematical ability between those at the extremes of the ability range. Even among first-class honours graduates the number of questions in an examination adequately attempted by the best first-class candidate may well be two or, even, three times as many as the bottom first-class candidate. Although both are given the same class, the examiners and their teachers know full well that there are considerable differences between them. Whether or not this is accurately captured by the normal distribution is a moot point but it certainly does not correspond to the kind of picture presented by the rectangular distribution. I repeat that it is difficult to know whether this feeling is empirically founded or not, but it certainly hints at the reasons why we feel more comfortable with normal distributions when trying to describe variation in something like human ability.

There is no likelihood of the Bell Curve being banished from the world of intelligence testing. As long as the tests involved require the adding up of scores, the central limit theorem will ensure that a degree of normality is induced. At the more fundamental level of the underlying g, there are good reasons for regarding the normal distribution as a good basis for constructing g-scores but this must be seen essentially as a convention, rather than a scientific fact. This is covered in chapter 10. When we come to compare groups, it is especially important to avoid the inconsistency of attributing normality to both the combined populations and the groups which make it up. We return to this in chapter 11.

10   What is g?

Introduction

At last we can focus on g itself. It cannot be directly observed because g is a latent variable, and so we also need to find some empirical substitute for it. This is the so-called g-score.

If it is really true that there is very little we can know about the form of the distribution of g, it is imperative that we consider the implications of this before we go any further. This is all the more important because the fact is not widely understood in the psychometric community, where it is not unusual to find talk of 'estimating' the distribution of the latent variable. Doing this invariably involves importing, inadvertently perhaps, some assumption to make it possible. There are a number of topics in intelligence testing, and latent variable modelling more generally, which depend on a distributional assumption for g. If such assumptions are not well-founded, we need to make an immediate assessment of the damage.

One aim of this chapter is, therefore, to look carefully at some of the properties of g and to see how far they depend upon the assumption made about its distribution. This will place our ultimate recommendation to use the g-score in preference to IQ on a more secure footing. A second aim is to discuss the validity, reliability and identity of g as a measure of general cognitive ability. The issues involved are deep and subtle and will require a good deal of patience and forbearance on the part of the reader. As a modest encouragement on the journey we may note, in advance, that we shall be able to do at least as well by pursuing the elusive g as if we had stayed with the more solid IQ. We shall try to lighten the exposition by using familiar analogies, but the reader must be prepared for a fairly sustained effort of concentration. We begin by approaching the whole question in a broader framework, illustrating why the distribution of g is so difficult to pin down.

A broader framework: latent structure models

In order to make our point we shall have to undertake what will appear to be a digression from the main theme, to look at what are called *latent structure models*. The factor model is an example of a latent structure model, but there are other kinds. In fact, the only difference between a factor model and other latent structure models lies in what they assume about the nature of the variables. Here we shall introduce one such latent structure model which differs from the factor model only in that it supposes the latent variables (factors) to be categorical rather than continuous. That is, individuals are supposed to be located in categories, which we cannot observe, instead of along a continuum. Latent structure models were introduced by Paul Lazarsfeld in the 1950s for use in sociology.[1] There are many practical situations where one suspects that individuals belong to one of several classes, or categories, which we are unable to observe directly. Thus, for example, one might suspect that firms could be classified according to how they conduct their labour relations.[2] In the simplest case one might postulate that firms could be classified according to whether they operate in an authoritative fashion or whether there is consultation with the workforce. It might not be possible or prudent to investigate this directly by visiting the firms and asking direct questions. Instead it might be much easier to circulate a questionnaire designed to elicit information on a good number of simple indicators which one might expect to be indicative of one or other management style. A latent class model is designed to tell us whether such a description fits. If it does, the model could be used to predict the latent class to which any individual firm belongs.

Similar problems arise in medical diagnosis. A patient may or may not be suffering from a particular condition which cannot be diagnosed directly. The doctor therefore makes observations and carries out tests in the hope of being able to decide into which class the patient falls. Again the only essential difference between this situation, and the one which we face in factor analysis, lies in the character of the latent variable. Whereas in factor analysis we suppose it to be continuous, in latent structure analysis we assume it to be categorical.

In practice, however, it is extremely difficult to distinguish empirically between the latent class model and the factor model. Thus, suppose we had successfully fitted a two-class latent structure model to a set of correlations of the kind to which we might otherwise have fitted a factor model. It turns out that we could have found a factor model, with only one factor, which would have fitted the correlations equally well. If the set of correlations were from real data, we would therefore have been quite unable to distinguish one model from the other. A similar result is true if we had fitted a latent structure model with more than two classes. A three-class model, for example, could be matched exactly with a two-factor model. This is a rather disconcerting discovery. It means that whenever a factor model has been successfully fitted, an equally good fit could have been obtained with a latent structure model and *vice versa*.[3] Since many thousands, if not millions, of factor models have been fitted over the years, the ramifications of this conclusion are far from trivial. It makes one pause to

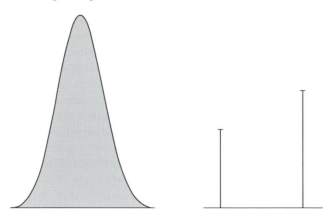

Figure 10.1 A normal distribution and a 'two-point' distribution for a latent variable.

wonder why some of the vast amount of effort expended by the intelligence testing industry has, to all appearances, *not* gone into considering the possibility that people might be classified into groups, on the basis of their intelligence, rather than being spread out along a continuum. After all, such groupings were part of the vocabulary in the early days when morons, idiots, imbeciles and so forth were defined as categories on the scale of intelligence. Even today, the 'educationally sub-normal' and the 'gifted' are sometimes spoken of as distinct categories.

We need to explore this matter further because it has important implications for our understanding of what it means to say that the distribution of g is indeterminate. The position may be illustrated by a simple diagram as in figure 10.1. The left-hand part of the figure shows the by-now familiar Bell Curve, alias the normal distribution. This is the form we typically assume when doing factor analysis. In particular it is the distribution that is usually assumed when we come to the scaling of g. The right-hand part of the figure shows a distribution, consisting of two spikes. These spikes correspond to latent classes and their heights are proportional to the sizes of those classes. This is, therefore, a rudimentary frequency distribution expressing the fact that, in the latent class model, individuals fall into one of the two classes with particular frequencies. The claim that we were making above is that, if we have a correlation table for a set of continuous indicators, we shall not be able to distinguish between a one-factor model, with a distribution for g which takes the normal form on the left, and a latent class model which specifies a distribution for g like that on the right. For that matter, it would be virtually impossible to distinguish either of these distributions from almost any other that we might care to specify.

Should we then abandon entirely any attempt to construct a scale of measurement for *g* on the grounds that the result would be arbitrary? There are two responses which can be made to this question. First, we can point to the fact that many other quantities, like length, do often have continuous distributions which appear similar to the Bell Curve. In the last chapter we saw how the normality of quantities, like human height, might result from the fact that height is determined by a large number of genes and other environmental influences, all of which are, individually, small. If, therefore, *g* were an indicator of a physical property or process of the brain, its value might well be determined by a great many genes and other influences, making its distribution somewhere close to normal. Although we do not, at the moment, have enough knowledge to know whether *g* actually does correspond to some physical property of the brain, it is not unreasonable to proceed on this assumption in anticipation of the day when it might have a more secure basis. In brief, we are saying that there is some indirect, if not direct, evidence for treating *g* as a continuous normal variable. Even if this anticipation is not fulfilled, we shall still be able to fall back on the second response.

This second response is the one we have made in the preceding chapter by arguing that the choice of a distribution for *g* does not need to be empirically based since it can never be observed, even indirectly. Any choice is then merely a matter of *convention*. To anticipate slightly, the scores we assign to individuals would be those which an individual at their rank order position would have had *if the distribution was, indeed, normal*. In other words, the normal distribution is part of the construction which determines what kind of a scale we have chosen to use. There is no objection to introducing such a convention provided that we always remember that that is just what it is. It means that we should not carry out any further analysis which depends on that assumption about the form of the distribution. We now look at this matter as it arises when we try to 'estimate' *g*.

Factor (or *g*-)scores

Having decided that we are going to measure *g* on a normally distributed scale (or any other for that matter) we next have to consider how to place individuals on that scale. In factor analysis this is known as the *problem of factor scores*.[4] The reader should be warned that some writers refer to the unobservable value of *g* as the factor score. This practice is unnecessary and confusing. A factor score is simply the scale value which we assign to an individual. Since we are here concerned with a scale we have labelled *g*, it is more natural to call the number a '*g*-score'. We have already introduced the term '*g*-factor' in chapter 5; now we have to consider how its value should be determined for any particular individual.

The natural way to proceed is to work out where an individual would be expected to be found on the scale, if the population distribution of g were standard normal. One way of doing this is to compute what is called the *expected value* of the latent variable, given the set of observed indicators. An expected value is simply the average of the values the quantity takes in repeated sampling. These expected values, or something very close to them, are usually given as part of the standard output of a factor analysis program.[5] It often turns out that the expectation, the g-score, is related to the indicator values for an individual in a rather simple way. When that happens, all we have to do is to multiply each indicator by an appropriate coefficient derived from the standard factor analysis routine and add up the resulting products, just as in the case of a principal component. Even in more complicated cases, this same sum is often the main part of the calculation. This sum shows very clearly how much each item contributes to the factor score – a matter to which we shall return in the following section.

There is a slightly different way of computing a g-score which brings in the normal distribution at the last stage instead of the first. In chapter 6 we approached factor analysis from a number of angles. One of these utilised the idea of what we called *sufficiency*. Its purpose was to group individuals in such a way that, within each group, the indicators were mutually independent. Since interdependence was assumed to have been caused by variation in one or more factors, it followed that the removal of correlation implied the removal of variation in the factors. In turn, this meant that each group was characterised by the fact that the factors were constant within that group. If, therefore, we can find some function(s) which are constant within that group, that function may be said to contain all the information in the indicators about the factors. (A function is anything which can be calculated from a set of numbers.) Thus, for example, if the sum of the indicators was approximately constant within each group, but different between groups, then the sum would contain all that the data have to tell us about the single underlying factor. In the language of chapter 6, the sum would be sufficient for g. In particular, the sum could be used to rank individuals according to their location on the scale of g. Using this approach we end up with a set of numbers, on the basis of which we can rank individuals. The spacing between these numbers, we recall, tells us nothing about the spacing between individuals. Having done this, however, there is nothing to prevent us adjusting the spacings to make them match the normal spacings. That is, for example, the individual who ranks thirteenth should be given the score of the thirteenth member of a sample, of the same size, from a normal distribution.

Either way, the resulting g-score depends critically on the form of the distribution we choose for g. Any subsequent calculations we make with the g-scores will similarly depend on that assumption. This arbitrariness might seem to put

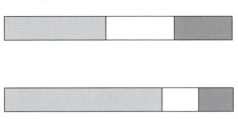

Figure 10.2 Illustrating how the composition of an indicator may vary. In the second case the indicator is more strongly influenced by the dominant factor.

the *g*-score at a disadvantage compared with IQ, until we remember that *its* distribution is equally arbitrary.

Factor loadings

In the last section we were concerned with how the *g*-scores depended on the indicators. In this section we reverse the position and look at how the indicators depend upon the factor, *g*. This has nothing to do with measuring *g* but it provides an alternative way of interpreting the factor, that is with deciding whether it can properly be regarded as a measure of general cognitive ability. The factor model itself says what the *form* of the dependence is, but for our present purposes we need to be able to quantify the relationship. The situation can easily be visualised and figure 10.2 has been constructed for this purpose.

In the upper part of the figure the magnitude of an indicator is represented by a long thin rectangle. It is divided into three parts, each representing a different contribution to the value of the indicator. The left-hand segment represents the contribution of the dominant factor, *g*, to the indicator. In this particular case it accounts for about half of the value of the indicator. The second segment represents the contribution of all other factors which, in the intelligence testing context, will typically be fairly small. Here they are shown as contributing about half as much as *g*. The remaining segment represents all other contributions which are specific to this particular indicator and are distinct from the factors. In the lower part of figure 10.2 the proportions have been varied. The segment representing *g*, at the left-hand end, now accounts for about three-quarters of the indicator's value. The other two segments are correspondingly smaller.

Pictures like this, or their equivalents in numbers, enable us to distinguish between indicators according to how important they are as indicators of *g*. An indicator like the second one in figure 10.2 is more strongly influenced by *g* than is the first one and it is, therefore, a better indicator. Another way of describing the second indicator is to say that it is a *purer* indicator of *g*, since it is less contaminated by other factors and extraneous sources of variation. Yet another way of putting the same point is to say that *g* has a larger *loading* in the second case than in the first. The larger the left-hand segment, the higher the loading g has.

These loadings are extremely useful when it comes to identifying and interpreting the factors. They enable us to see more clearly what it is that the factor is measuring. In our earlier discussions we noted that, if all the indicators were positively correlated with one another, this could be taken as an indication that they all depended upon a common underlying factor. That rough interpretation took no account of the fact that some indicators might have been better than others. We are now able to remedy this deficiency with the help of the factor loadings.

Ideally, we would like to have a set of indicators all having a high loading on g. Each indicator would then be a relatively pure indicator of g and the set of indicators, taken together, would provide a fairly clear picture of what it was that g was measuring. In practice, the loadings will vary and the differences between them lead us towards a more refined interpretation of the factors. For example, in the items used in standard IQ tests, like the Wechsler battery, it is found that certain items load more heavily on g than others. In particular, items known as Raven's Matrices have a high loading on g and so are particularly good indicators of g. This type of item has no verbal content but depends on the perception of spatial patterns. It may therefore be assumed to be less influenced by cultural or educational background than the kind of items which have to be expressed in words, or which appeal to concepts current in a particular culture. This suggests that items like Raven's Matrices may be good indicators of pure intellectual ability and therefore that a good index of g might be constructed from items of this kind. In any case, focusing on items with high loadings will enable us to refine our interpretation of the factor and so get closer to what g actually measures.

We could do exactly the same kind of thing, starting with the factor scores which, we saw, showed us how a given factor was influenced by the items. Those items with large coefficients, which contribute more to the factor, are therefore better indicators of what the factor is measuring. In certain special cases these two different approaches turn out to be equivalent, but even when they are not, they are doing essentially the same kind of thing.

Next we turn away from the measure itself and examine its properties; in particular its *validity* and *reliability*. These are the two criteria against which any measure has to be judged.

Validity

Validity is the most important criterion used in judging a measure. It is concerned with whether the index measures what it was designed to measure. When constructing something like an index of industrial production, we would be asking whether the index does, indeed, measure industrial production satisfactorily. In the present case this idea does not translate so readily into the field of intelligence because we are here looking at something, called *g*, which has emerged from factor analysis, rather than being deliberately constructed by ourselves in the manner used for IQ. What we are really interested in, of course, is whether this new measure, produced by factor analysis, could serve as a measure of intelligence, in some acceptable sense.

The validity of a measure is usually judged by comparing it with another measure which is already firmly established. Such a measure might be termed the 'gold standard'. A moment's reflection will convince us that this criterion is bordering on the absurd, at least in the case of the attempt to measure intelligence. Why would we be trying to construct a new measure if we already had a perfectly good one at our disposal? This may be putting the matter a little unfairly, since some measures may be more convenient in some situations than others, but the main point stands. In fact, the question of the identity of *g* discussed below, would be redundant if a gold standard existed since all we would have to see is how each new candidate measured up to the standard. In practice we shall not have a single definitive alternative measure against which to judge the validity of any prospective *g*; there will usually be a whole cluster of such '*g*'s which appear to be more or less the same. If all such candidates are correlated positively among themselves, then we may have some confidence that they have a common reference, and this confidence is increased in proportion to the number of corroborating comparisons that we make. In brief, validity has to be achieved by mutual support rather than by an absolute test.

However, there is more to judging validity than 'internal' comparisons of one candidate with another. It is often recommended that one should also look for other manifest indicators which one is confident reflect intelligence. Any valid measure should correlate positively with them. If there are, indeed, quantities around, like the number of years of schooling, which tell us something about an individual's intelligence, why are they not being incorporated into the new measure itself? If there is relevant material to hand, surely we should use as much of it as possible to improve the quality of the new measure that we are constructing?

In any case, we have already noted an element of circularity in the whole exercise. We are proposing to judge the quality of a new measure against other variables, whether latent of manifest, which are certainly no better, and probably less, well founded. The whole process is reminiscent of trying to pull oneself up by one's own bootlaces.

In the present context, at least, the traditional approach to judging validity starts from the wrong end. It begins by asking whether the index which we have constructed is an adequate measure of intelligence. We should start at the other end, by taking the measure which has emerged from factor analysis and asking what name we can most meaningfully give to what it appears to be measuring. That is, the exercise is one of naming a measure, rather than judging its conformity to some previously determined concept.

We have indicated above, in the section on factor loadings, how this naming process can be carried out with the help of the loadings. The important question with g, therefore, is: is 'intelligence' or, perhaps, 'general intelligence' or 'general cognitive ability', an appropriate name to give to the dominant factor which emerges from the factor analysis of most large and varied sets of test items of general ability? The general consensus emerging from the great multitude of such analyses which have been carried out is that the term 'general intelligence' does provide a reasonable description of what the dominant factor, called g, is measuring. The fact that the largest loadings turn out to be on those items which seem to test 'pure' ability, rather than on those involving verbal skills (and hence with some risk of cultural contamination), may be used to support this conclusion.

It is clear that g is a narrower concept than the more fuzzy notion of intelligence which the classical pioneers of the IQ world set out to capture. We see this particularly in the fact that factor analysis of the items in the common IQ tests has revealed that they depend on several factors, of which g is only one, albeit the most important. The process of factor analysis has, therefore, separated this dominant dimension from the small cluster of other abilities which seem to be present in all the standard tests. Whether or not this single dimension is more useful in practice is an empirical matter.

In our earlier discussion of measuring intelligence, we spoke of a dialogue with the data. The idea was that, as we had no precise idea of what this thing called intelligence really was, we should match any measure, which we had provisionally constructed, against the rather fuzzy context of meaning which had led to the selection of the original items. The first comparison would point out the direction in which to move to get the most appropriate items and so, by degrees, we could bring our index into agreement with the usage of the term 'intelligence' in common language. We have now moved somewhat beyond that by bringing factor analysis into the picture. We are still letting the data speak for themselves by pointing to the kind of items which are likely to load heavily on g. In this way we begin to get a clearer idea of what g really is. The validity of g is judged by whether the name given to the dominant factor is appropriate, rather than by whether the factor corresponds to some pre-determined definition. The whole process expresses in a more formal way what we were searching for earlier.

However, we want rather more than a valid measure of general intelligence. A valid measure based on only two or three items might be a pure indicator of g but, being based on such a small number of items, would be very imprecise. The question of the precision of a measure brings us to the question of *reliability*.

Reliability

It is a curious fact that the notion of reliability figures very prominently in item response theory, where the indicators are usually binary, but hardly at all in factor analysis. Nevertheless, it is just as important to know how precise is our knowledge of *g* when the indicators are continuous as when they are categorical. We are familiar with the idea that an average calculated from a large sample gives a more precise estimate than one from a small sample. We would expect the same to be true when sampling indicators. That is, the more items we include in the test, the better the measure of intelligence. This is broadly true although the position is rather more complicated. Generally speaking, the more items we have the better will be our measure, but some items are worth more than others. We have just seen that some items are 'purer' indicators of *g* than others. Other things being equal, it is therefore better to add such items to the battery rather than those which contain a more modest component of *g*. However, there is a risk in multiplying the number of items in a test battery indiscriminately. Once we have 'used up', as it were, all the obvious items which load heavily on *g*, there will be a tendency for new items to contribute less on *g* and more on new factors and so make the interpretation more difficult. At the other extreme, new items may be so like the old that they add virtually nothing. This is particularly likely to be the case with items of a simple arithmetical kind where, once one has got the idea, the mere repetition of similar items will reveal little that is new about the ability being tested.

There are at least two ways of assessing the reliability of a measuring instrument derived from factor analysis. One is to calculate by how much the variability (usually measured by the variance or standard deviation of the measure) would be reduced if we actually knew the true value of *g*. If there is a drastic reduction, that is tantamount to saying that the score contains a great deal of information about *g* because, once we know *g*, there is very little uncertainty about the *g*-score. Conversely, if knowing *g* would hardly affect our uncertainty about the score, it cannot be said that there is much in common between the two. We are thus determining the gain in precision which comes from knowing *g*.

It seems rather perverse to base a measure of reliability on the effect of knowing something which, in the nature of the case, we can never know. A more direct approach is simply to calculate the standard deviation of the (unknown) *g*, given the data we have on the individual. This is the obvious next step to take after finding the *g*-score. The latter is the expected value, or mean value of *g*, given the data and the reliability is then measured by the standard deviation. This calculation is perfectly feasible. Standard deviations obtained by this method often turn out to be surprisingly large showing that, even though we may have a measure made up of impeccably chosen items, they do not fix the value of *g* at all precisely.

The identity of *g*

Next we come to a rather tricky question. If *g* is the fundamental measure of general ability, its influence should be revealed whenever and wherever appropriate tests are administered. But, even supposing that a single dominant dimension of latent variation appears, whatever precise collection of items is used and whether they are applied to Indians or Australians, what justification is there for believing that it is the same '*g*' which turns up each time? There is no 'standard *g*' kept in a laboratory somewhere which can be wheeled out to authenticate the latest arrival. The best we can do is to compare one candidate with another.

Suppose, first of all, that we had administered the *same* set of items to samples drawn from two *different* populations, English and Australian, for example. Suppose also that we are satisfied, as a result of factor analysis in each case, that there is a single common underlying factor in each population. What grounds do we have for supposing that the factors uncovered in the two populations are, in fact, the same? If they are indeed the same, we would expect the loadings on each item to be much the same in the two countries – or, at any rate, proportional. A measure of their similarity is provided by something called the *coefficient of colligation* which is, in essence, a correlation between the two sets of loadings. Another way of looking at the problem is to think in terms of sufficient statistics. We would expect the same sufficient statistic to emerge in each case (remembering that 'same' here means that one must be a transformation of the other). Looked at in yet another way, if we were to pool the two samples, we would still expect to find that one factor was sufficient to account for the correlations. The sufficient statistic should then be much the same as we find for either population separately. The approximate identity of the two candidates for *g* would then be checked by seeing whether they resulted from essentially the same sufficient statistic.

Alternatively, suppose that we stick to the same sample of subjects, but administer two different sets of items to members each purporting to depend on the same latent variable. If, again, one factor appears to be adequate in each case, how do we decide whether it is the *same* factor? In this case we cannot compare the loadings, or the sufficient statistic, because there are no variables in common. However, if the dominant factors in each case are indicative of the same underlying *g*, they should rank the common set of individuals in the same order. In other words, their identity can be checked by looking at how closely correlated are the rankings in the two populations. If the correlation is high, we can be confident that the two factors are close even if not identical.

If we try to go even further than this and compare samples from two populations, where there is no overlap of either subjects or items, there is no formal comparison which can be made. Informally, we might feel that the items were very similar in character and that the subjects were sampled from similar populations. In that case a similar factor structure would be indicative of a common *g* in both cases.

IQ versus *g*

As we move towards the end of the book we must confront again the question which has been just below the surface ever since we drew attention to the two main strands which make up the history of intelligence testing. On the one hand there is the path which led to the various indices of the general intelligence which we can conveniently describe as IQ measures. These were constructed from selections of test items proposed by their inventors, because, collectively, they appeared to encompass the kind of tasks which an intelligent person ought to be able to carry out. Essentially they were averages of scores on the items. On the other hand there is what we have called the model-based approach, using factor analysis, which has led to the unobservable quantity called *g*. Although we have already expressed a strong preference for *g*, we have kept both of these balls in the air, sometimes giving prominence to one and sometimes to the other. This has been partly a matter of necessity because much of the research on intelligence has been based on IQ. For example the discussion of heritability, to which we come in chapter 12, has almost exclusively been concerned with the inheritance of IQ. At this stage, however, we have arrived at a position from which we have a better view of the issues and are better placed to assess the relative merits of these two approaches.

Let us say unequivocally at the outset that, for scientific purposes, *g* is much to be preferred. Many of the disputes with which the discussion of intelligence has been riven stem from the subjective and somewhat arbitrary character of the IQ measure. As factor analysis has shown, the items which go into a typical measure of IQ cannot be adequately summarised by a single one-dimensional factor. This is an important scientific finding and immediately enables us to agree with those who criticise supporters of IQ on the grounds that they treat it as a unitary one-dimensional source of variation (in reality, they rarely do). The fact that IQ depends upon more than one factor has some important consequences, especially when we wish to compare the intelligence of different groups. The difference between males and females illustrates the point very well, even if it is not large enough to be of very much practical importance. The well-attested fact that men tend to perform better on those items which have a spatial content, whereas women are stronger on verbal items, immediately shows that the advantage can be shifted towards males or females by changing the composition of the battery of test items. Including more verbal items will tend to make women appear more intelligent than men. This would not be possible if the test batteries were measuring a single latent variable. The same kind of considerations apply in many other comparisons, not least to the more important question of whether there are intelligence differences between ethnic groups.

The real weakness, however, of measures like IQ is the arbitrariness of the selection of test items. Since we start without any precise idea of what it is that we are trying to measure, there is, inevitably, an arbitrariness about the pool of test items on which our measure is based. But the fact that some items may be culturally biased has fanned the flames of many a fierce argument about ethnic comparisons. We have suggested that the problem is less acute if we freely recognise at the outset, that it is only by a process of dialogue with the data that we converge on an acceptable fit between the data and the concept. This reduces, but does not eliminate, the arbitrariness and it cannot completely overcome the problem of fuzziness in the initial concept.

The second approach, leading to g, is not entirely devoid of arbitrariness but its role is much smaller. Here we specify general relationships between the set of items which we choose and the latent variables which we suppose are responsible for their correlations. We then allow the data to determine how many such variables are needed and which among them captures the principal source of variation. It is true that the initial selection of items has to be made by reference to what we understand intelligence to be but, provided that the set is large and varied enough, any factor representing general intellectual ability should emerge. It is rather like casting a net into the sea in the hope of catching the most common sort of fish. If we are primarily after one particular variety, we may be more successful by casting in one direction rather than another, but providing that the fish are reasonably numerous and well dispersed, we should certainly catch some from any casting. If the area over which we cast is large enough, we can hardly fail to make a reasonable catch. Similarly, if we initially choose a wide enough range of items when constructing a test, we should certainly find enough of them loading heavily on the major dimension of variability to identify the main factor. Some arbitrariness remains because there will always be potential disagreement about which items should be included, but the method itself will determine for us which are the important items and which are not. Furthermore, we are guaranteed to get a one-dimensional measure.

Having said all of this, the fact that g cannot be directly observed seems to wipe out all the other advantages which we have claimed for it. The day is saved by the fact that, although we cannot observe g, we can make an estimate of it (the g-score) and, in addition, say something about the precision of that estimate. We end up, therefore, with something not very different from an IQ measure, because it often turns out to be a weighted average of the item scores and therefore superficially hardly distinguishable from an IQ measure. The difference, and this is crucial, is that the measure is genuinely one-dimensional and we can say something precise about its reliability. If it also turns out to be readily identifiable with the popular understanding of what general intelligence is, its superiority over IQ is confirmed.

What then is *g*? *g* is a human construct designed to capture the essence of the widely used notion of general intelligence. It is constructed within a framework, depending on the logic of probability theory, which ensures that its properties can be rigorously investigated. This theory exposes the inherent limitations of the measurement process. In particular, that the most we can do in practice is to rank individuals according to their estimated level of *g*. The usefulness of the concept rests on a vast amount of empirical evidence that the dimension of human ability, which we call *g*, emerges whenever the results of a sufficiently broad range of tests of mental ability are analysed. The great weakness of *g* is that it is only an indirect measure of the brain activity on which mental performance ultimately depends. Until a satisfactory method of expressing human mental abilities in terms of what goes on in the brain becomes available, *g* will have a useful role to play. It is far from ideal but it is the best measure we have.

11   Are some groups more intelligent than others?

The big question

Here we move into one of the most contentious areas of all. Much of the debate which followed the publication of *The Bell Curve* took place over the question of whether American whites were inherently more intelligent than blacks and, though with rather less fervour, whether those of Asian origin were more intelligent than either. Differences across time have also attracted attention. It appears that IQ has increased in many parts of the world over the last few generations – the so-called Flynn effect. These simple sounding statements conceal fundamental questions about whether it is possible to compare groups at all. We have seen that measures of intelligence are defined relative to a particular population. How then can it be possible to make comparisons between populations? This is the question that this chapter seeks to explore. The going will not always be easy but, as we have said before, getting to the bottom of the arguments is essential if we wish to take part in the debate.

Although we speak of one group being more intelligent than another, we already know that such statements cannot be given a precise meaning. Intelligence is multidimensional and this fact prevents us from even ranking individuals unambiguously. The question will have to be worded in terms of some quantity which can be expressed on a one-dimensional scale. If g is that fundamental underlying quantity, we would ideally like to be able to say, for example, that there is no difference between the average g levels of young adults today and those of twenty years ago. But since we cannot observe g directly, it is not immediately obvious how to do this. Instead, therefore, we shall begin with those quantities for which a precise numerical value can be calculated and return to g later. The g-score is the obvious substitute for g but almost all published work on the subject relates to IQ. In any case, g and IQ are highly correlated. Our discussion will, therefore, be in terms of IQ but much of what we say will apply equally to g-scores or, indeed, any other index calculated from test scores.

Group differences

The idea that individuals differ in their intelligence, however it is quantified, is implicit in the very concept itself. For if all individuals had identical intelligence the concept would be redundant. Intelligence is a source of variation and variation means difference, but talk of *group* differences is another thing entirely. Here we are asking whether members of one racial group, for example, are, in some sense, more intelligent than those of another. The confusion which underlies much of the debate about group differences is not something peculiar to latent variables such as *g* or, indeed, manifest quantities like IQ. It concerns a basic and elementary statistical principle which is called into play so often that one would have expected it to be well understood, but the literature of this area shows otherwise. As in some previous chapters, we shall begin by clarifying the issues at stake using a simple example which has nothing to do with intelligence testing. Having got the principles clear, we can then return to our main concern.

Let us first consider what is involved in saying that two groups differ in some attribute. To make the matter as uncontentious as possible, let us consider again the matter of human height. Nothing is more obvious than that individuals differ in their height, some are short and some are tall. Sometimes, however, we may wish to make group comparisons as, for example, when we want to say that men tend to be taller than women. We are certainly not saying that all men are taller than all women for that is obviously not true. In making a group comparison, we are extending the notion of height to be a descriptor of a group rather than of an individual. We are thus back to the important concept of a *collective property* of a group as distinct from an *individual property* of a person. The only difference here is that we are talking about a group of *individuals* rather than a group of *variables*. Usually we make group comparisons of this kind, using something like the *average* height, without thinking too much about the logic of what we are doing. That is, we add up the individual heights, divide them by their number, and produce a measure of height which applies to the group rather than to any individual within it. We have already discussed the distinction between an average, which applies to a group, and the value for a single individual by reference to an average family of 1.6 children. The average in that case was a measure which applied to families in general and not to any particular family. When we say that men tend to be taller than women we are making a statement about a collective property and not about any particular couple.

Such collective measures of a population do not tell the whole story, of course. The arithmetic average is only one of several measures which can be used to characterise the magnitude of some quantity in a population. One other commonly used measure is the median. The median height is the point on the scale such that half the members of a population are taller and the other half are shorter. It is conceivable that in making a comparison between two populations the average will point in one direction and the median in another. However, such fine distinctions are likely to be insignificant in the present context and so we shall ignore them.

It is more important to note that populations can also be described by other collective characteristics. The dispersion, or spread, of height may be even more important for some purposes. Two populations with precisely the same average height may differ in that one has many more people at the two extremes than the other. In making the statement that men tend to be taller than women we are saying something which can be justified by reference to averages, but which certainly does not exhaust all there is to be said about the differences between the distributions of height in the two populations.

Group differences may, of course, be more subtle than in the simple situation which we have outlined above. Chinese tend to be shorter than Scandinavians. Women tend to be shorter than men. But these statements do not immediately tell us whether Chinese men tend to be shorter or taller than Scandinavian women. It will often be necessary to classify members of a population, or cross-classify them, in a number of ways and the pattern of differences between groups may be quite complicated. Apparent differences between groups on one variable may, in fact, arise because that variable is itself highly correlated with a second variable which is more fundamental.

Examples of group differences

The main sort of difference we had in mind above was between the general level of height in the two groups, though we noted that there might be other differences – in dispersion, for example. We need to set out exactly what group comparisons involve. In essence we wish to compare particular characteristics of frequency distributions. We have already met the idea of a frequency distribution in chapter 9 mainly represented by the normal distribution – or to use Herrnstein and Murray's term, the Bell Curve. Here the focus shifts to comparing distributions. The Bell Curve will continue to be at the centre but it is important to remember that other quantities have distributions with different shapes. Figure 11.1 shows, again, what the Bell Curve looks like but this time three such distributions have been superimposed. Because the distribution is symmetrical, the average is in the centre. As the average changes, we can imagine the distribution moving bodily to the left or right as shown in figure 11.1. Figure 11.2(a) illustrates the position when two such distributions are compared. The lower distribution has a larger mean than the upper, but otherwise the distributions are the same. The groups represented by these distributions differ in their mean level, which is the kind of thing we would expect to find if we

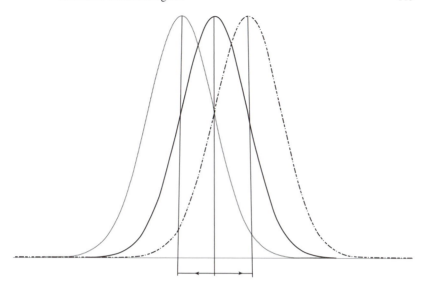

Figure 11.1 Showing how a shift in the location of the distribution indicates a shift in the whole distribution.

were comparing the heights of men and women. There is considerable overlap and if, for example, we look at the point on the upper scale marked A, there would be men whose height lies below this point even though this is below the women's average. In this example the lower group has a larger average height although there is a considerable overlap in the two distributions. Figure 11.2(b) shows a different situation in which there is also a group difference, but this time it is in the spread rather than the location. Both distributions have the same average but, in the lower example, there are more individuals at either extreme. In figure 11.2(c) there is a difference in both location and spread. Finally, in figure 11.2(d), we have two distributions with the same location and spread, but differing shapes.

These examples make it clear that group differences can manifest themselves, simultaneously, in many ways. It is important to be clear whether any differences we report relate only to location or to other aspects of the distribution as well.

Group differences in IQ

These considerations apply as much to IQ as to height or anything else of the same kind. To say that one group, one race for example, has a higher IQ than another is not to say that all members of the former are more intelligent than all those of the latter group. Yet one does not have to search for very long in the more polemical parts of the literature to get this impression.[1] In some cases the

(a)

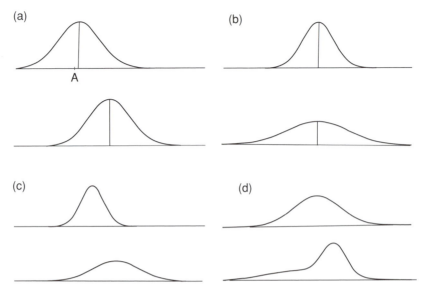

A

(b)

(c)

(d)

Figure 11.2 (a) Comparison of location when spread and shape are the same. (b) Comparison of spread when location and shape are the same. (c) Normal distributions with different locations and different spreads. (d) Two distributions with the same location and spread but different shape.

error goes even deeper by implying that the differences in IQ imply differences in human worth as, for example, when it is said that the analysis shows that one race is inferior to another. What such claims usually mean is that the average of one group is larger than the other while the spread and the shape remain the same. In other words, that the situation is as illustrated in figure 11.2(a).

In the case of IQ, however, it is not quite as simple as that. IQ is not a straightforward average of a set of scores and so we are not comparing frequency distributions of scores. We are comparing averages of distributions that have been standardised, that is, distributions which have already been transformed so as to make their averages 100 and their standard deviations (measures of spread) 15. So the comparison is pointless! To emphasise this, imagine that we have scores for two countries, Lilliput and Laputa. In both countries batteries of test items have been constructed, appropriate to their own cultures and in their own languages but on the same principles. Frequency distributions are drawn up, scaled in such a manner as to make their averages 100 and their standard deviations 15. The method of calculation also ensures that the distributions have the Bell Curve shape. What can be said about differences between the two countries? Absolutely nothing, because the method of calculating IQ in each country from the raw scores determines in advance what the average, spread and shape of the distributions will be. We know in advance what the answer will be so the whole exercise is meaningless!

How then does it come about, that the literature is full of claims such as that American whites have higher IQs, on average, than American blacks? The difference quoted is usually about fifteen points. It cannot mean that whites and blacks have been treated as two separate populations in the manner described above or their averages would have turned out to be the same. Equally puzzling is the claim, sometimes encountered, that IQ has increased over time. This cannot mean that each new cohort has been treated as a distinct population. On what basis then can claims about group differences be made?

In order to get our thinking straight on how to make group comparisons, we must bring another element into the discussion. This is the set of test items. When imagining the comparison of IQ in Lilliput and Laputa we explicitly assumed that it would not be possible to use the same set of items in each country. All that was required was that the sets of items were judged to be equivalent in the sense that they were indicators of intelligence. This meant that there was no way of calibrating the items to make the scores obtained in the two countries comparable. All that we could do was to make comparisons between individuals within each population. However, suppose that Lilliput and Laputa are regions of the same country with a common language and culture. Would it then be possible to compare the average scores in the two regions by using the same items and so see whether or not there was a group difference? Yes, it would be possible and, after making due allowance for the effect of any sampling error, we could say with confidence which region had the higher average IQ. However, this is not quite what we want because the differences quoted in the literature are expressed, not in terms of actual scores, but on an IQ scale – as fifteen points, for example. How do we convert the difference between two averages to units of IQ? The short answer is that we cannot do so without making some assumptions. However, before spelling out what they are, it is worth pausing to consider why we find ourselves in this position. After all, there is no problem about comparing average heights. What is it that distinguishes test scores from measures of height?

The difficulty arises from the nature of the measurements involved in the two cases. Height and IQ are different kinds of measure (see the section on *levels of measurement* in chapter 5). Height is a length. The scale of length has a natural zero point and two lengths can be compared by laying the objects side by side. If we wish, we can express their lengths as multiples of some standard length, like the foot or metre. There can be no argument about whether one rod is longer or shorter than another. The same cannot be said of test scores or their averages. There is, in general, no natural zero point and so the position of any individual on the scale can only be judged relative to others from the same population. It was this feature of Wechsler's version of the Intelligence

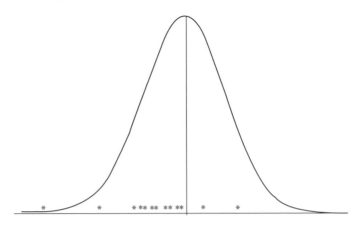

Figure 11.3 Typical locations of black Americans on scale of white Americans.

Quotient which worried his critics because the use of a relative measure ruled out from the start many important comparisons which one might wish to make.

The easiest way to see what is involved is to take an example and the case of black and white Americans serves the purpose admirably. The early work on IQ in the USA was done on white Americans, and on large numbers at that. Their IQs were calculated by reference to the distribution of scores in that population. When the same test was applied to black Americans there were two options for converting them to IQs. One would have been to treat them as a separate population and to standardise their scores using the average and standard deviation estimated for the black population. As we have seen above, this would not have served the purpose because it would have yielded a distribution with the same average and standard deviation as the whites. The other alternative was to treat the black sample as if they came from a distribution which was the same as the whites except, possibly, for its average. In that case the standardisation would be done using the white standard deviation and that would lead to IQs on the same scale as the whites. The assumptions, to which we referred a moment ago, are that the distributions for the two groups have the same spread and shape. The latter assumption is likely to be satisfied, approximately at least, because averages tend to have bell-shaped distributions, but it is less obvious that the same will be true for the spreads. There is little evidence in the literature that this question has received the attention it deserves.[2]

The position has been illustrated in figure 11.3. The distribution represents the distribution of IQs for white Americans. The horizontal scale could be expressed in terms of IQs or of the untransformed scores. This does not affect the shape of the distribution but only the labelling. The asterisks are intended to mark the locations of typical black Americans. They have been positioned to have an average level at around 85 on the whites' IQ scale. On this basis we could legitimately report an IQ difference of about fifteen points. But it is important to notice that the standardisation has been done by reference to the whites' distribution. In effect we are asking: if this sample of blacks had been drawn from the white population what would their IQs have been?

To see why this might be important, consider what the position would have been if the asterisks had shown a much wider scatter. (As it is, they were placed so as to have about the same spread as the whites' distribution.) Their IQs, as read off from the whites' scale, would have been more widely scattered. Conversely, suppose that we had started with a large black population, having a much larger spread than the whites, and had constructed the IQ scale by reference to that population. The whites would still have had the larger average IQ, but their scatter would have been much less because it would now be read off from the black IQ scale. This illustrates the role of the assumption that both populations have the same dispersion. If they do not, then it matters which one we use for standardisation.

The same point can be made by reference to another question of practical interest. Do males and females differ in IQ? Rose and Richardson both remark that the fact that they come out with the same average is an artefact of the method of calculation.[3] One can see how this would come about if they were treated as two distinct populations. In that case both populations would be assigned an average of 100 and equality of the sexes would be guaranteed! However, there are other ways of standardising the populations which will give different answers. There is not a great deal at stake because the differences are small however we do the calculation, but it is instructive to follow through the argument in order to show just how careful we need to be.

Taking the same route as above, we could start with the distributions of test scores for males and females. These would show whether or not there was a difference in average level. If we were then to go on to express them on a common scale of IQ, we should have the choice of doing this by reference to the male or the female distribution. If the standard deviations of the two distributions were much the same, the choice would not be critical. However we have already noted that the dispersion of test scores is greater for men than for women. This certainly seems to be the case for tests in mathematics, where men tend to appear disproportionately at the two extremes of the distribution. As our black and white example showed, the IQs assigned to the two groups would depend on which distribution we chose for standardisation. In that case the white group was very much larger and so it was natural to take it as defining the scale. In the case of males and females, where the groups are roughly equal in size, the choice is not so obvious.

This fact suggests a third alternative. Why not treat the males and females as a single population? All we would have to do is to calculate the IQs for all individuals, regardless of sex, and then ask whether the IQ scores assigned to females were, on average, different from those of the males. We would then have the answer that we were looking for expressed directly in units of IQ.

The answers obtained by these various methods would all be slightly different. Which one would be correct? There is no right answer to this question. They differ because the unit of IQ used in each case differs – and the units differ because the units are defined with respect to a particular population – and the populations also differ. We are asking more of the methodology than it is capable of delivering. We must learn to live within the limits imposed upon us by the framework we are compelled to use.

The Flynn effect

There are two types of comparison that we commonly wish to make between groups. One concerns differences between races, classes, sexes and so forth such as we have discussed above. The other concerns differences between the state of the same population at different times. It is certainly true, for example, that the mean IQ in some populations has increased substantially over the last twenty or thirty years. Does this imply that there have been changes in innate ability? Are today's children more intelligent than those of a generation ago or have other changes simply made them better at doing IQ tests? The short answer is that there is no way of knowing, for certain. We now go on to elaborate this rather cryptic answer.

Charting changes in IQ over time is essentially the same problem as comparing groups. The groups in this case are defined as the members of a particular population at a particular time. Thus one might look, for example, at the population of university students in a given country at ten-year intervals, applying the same test items in each group. The histograms of scores would reveal any trend over time. Extensive studies have been carried out in many countries and these all seem to show a steady and rather large rise over many decades. This has come to be referred to as the Flynn effect,[4] after the principal investigator of this phenomenon. Provided that the items themselves remain appropriate over the extended period (which is by no means certain) changes in the average score would be indicative of real changes in performance. What those changes actually signify is a question to which we shall come below. The validity of expressing changes over time in units of IQ again depends on whether the population distribution remains the same throughout the period in all respects, other than its location. Figure 11.4 illustrates two possible scenarios for studies carried out over three time periods. In the left-hand part of the figure everything about the distribution remains the same except for the average, which is

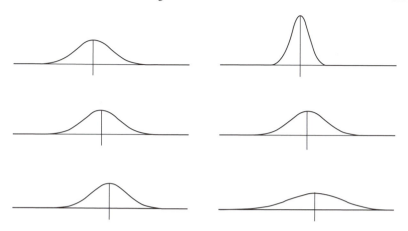

Figure 11.4 Showing how changes over time may differ. On the left-hand side only the location changes; on the right, location and spread change.

increasing. Here it would be legitimate to express the increments in units of IQ. The sequence in the right-hand part shows a change, not only in location, but also in spread. In this case it would not be possible to measure the increments in IQ units unless there were some powerful reason for adopting the unit derived from one particular year (the first one, perhaps).

Explaining group differences

Having established the existence of a group difference in IQ, the important questions concern what it means and whether it is possible or desirable to do anything to change the situation. If the difference is the result of innate mental ability which cannot be changed, one set of questions arises such as: how should society be organised to make the best of this state of affairs? If the difference is due to the varying economic, educational and social circumstances under which the two groups live, another set concerns how the lot of the deprived group can be brought up to the standard of the best. We know that IQ scores can be affected by many things, including cultural factors and, even, the amount of practice in doing the tests which the subject has had. As it is, we have to make do with IQ, which, at best, is contaminated by the effects of all sorts of extraneous factors. Is it, then, possible to disentangle these various factors and to see whether any group difference remains when the effects of all other factors are removed?

Sometimes we shall be able to identify factors which may contribute to group differences. For example, children who have had help at home in preparing for a test would be expected to do better than those who had no such help. In principle, such effects can be eliminated, or reduced, by ensuring that the groups are properly matched beforehand. The aim should be to control or eliminate as many extraneous factors as possible from the comparison which might contribute to the group difference.

The case for believing that an IQ difference was indicative of a real difference between the sexes would be progressively strengthened as first one and then another possible explanation was ruled out. The position is rather similar to that which arose over the relationship between smoking and cancer of the lung. It was early established that heavy smokers were more prone to succumb to cancer of the lung, but it did not follow from this that the higher death rate among smokers was caused by smoking. Smokers had other things in common like, for example, a greater likelihood of living or working in a polluted atmosphere which might have been the true cause. Only when such alternative explanations had been eliminated, by showing that the effect persisted when they were controlled, did it become increasingly clear what the true culprit was. Interestingly, it was suggested, notably by Sir Ronald Fisher, that there might be some innate genetic difference which pre-disposed some people to become smokers and also increased their cancer risk. From a strictly logical point of view, it is virtually impossible to rule out some remaining unknown factor which has escaped our attention. In the smoking example it was necessary to uncover the biochemical processes by which the action of smoke on the lung tissues could induce cancer that put the matter beyond reasonable doubt. Once this was done there was a causal theory explaining why tobacco smoke could cause cancer. No such causal theory is yet available linking race and intelligence and that is why our conclusions have to be so tentative. Only if we could make physical measurements on brain processes or other variables, known to determine g, would it be possible to be sure that ethnic differences contribute to differences in g and hence to the observed differences in IQ.

In the human sciences the problem of disentangling the effects of competing factors is ubiquitous. It is often impossible to control or eliminate extraneous factors completely. Equally, there are costs of doing nothing while awaiting a definitive answer. In practice we often have to make a judgement on incomplete evidence and be content with something short of certainty. When the effects of two, or more, factors cannot be separated they are said to be *confounded*. Confounding is such an important feature of research in intelligence that we shall digress for a moment to explore it further by extending the range of examples.

Confounding

Recent research in America seems to indicate that breathing second-hand smoke lowers the IQ of children.[5] Not that we could ever tell, of course, whether this was true of any particular child. There is no way we could know what the IQ of a child brought up in a non-smoking household would have been had the family smoked. What we can do is to make a group comparison between the average IQ of a representative sample of children exposed to second-hand smoke and a sample having no exposure. Suppose this shows, as it did in the study reported, that children exposed to a smoking atmosphere tend to have a lower IQ. Does it follow that 'passive' smoking leads to a reduction in IQ?

Critics have argued that this conclusion should be regarded with caution because there may be 'confounding' factors. This means that there may be other factors, so mixed up with passive smoking, that their effects cannot be separated. For example, it is known that children whose mothers smoked during pregnancy are also likely to have a lowered IQ – but mothers who smoke in the presence of their children are also likely to have smoked during pregnancy. This will not always be the case, but if the 'smoking during pregnancy' and the 'smoking during childhood' groups have a large degree of overlap, we shall not be able to tell whether the lowered IQ is the result of inhaling cigarette smoke as a child or of absorbing tobacco products from the mother's blood during pregnancy. The two factors are thus *confounded*.

Is there any way in which the individual effects can be separated in this case? If exposure to cigarette smoke was really having an effect, we would expect to observe it whether or not the mother had smoked during pregnancy. This could be checked if we were able to obtain two samples where the only way they differed was in the presence of one of the factors. Sometimes this can be done, but often it is impossible.

In reality, there will usually be many factors likely to produce the observed effect. In the smoking example one might observe that smokers are more common in the lower socioeconomic classes. Hence it could be that lack of intellectual stimulus, poorer diet, blood lead levels or schooling was really the villain of the piece. Because these factors are believed to lead to lowered IQ levels, it could be that the association with smoking, passive or otherwise, is illusory.

As we have noted, this situation is extremely common in the human sciences. Faced with the same problem in the experimental sciences, it is obvious what should be done. We would simply control the levels of all relevant factors in such a way that we could disentangle their individual effects. In an agricultural experiment on the effect of fertilisers, for example, we can apply a particular fertiliser to one plot of land and not to another and, if the plots are otherwise identical, regard the difference in the yields as a measure of the effect. Many fertilisers can be compared in this way if appropriate combinations are applied in the manner dictated by the theory of the design of experiments.

In the human sciences we can only rarely exercise such control. We have to make do with whatever society and nature happen to have selected for us. Since these things are not ordered for the convenience of social scientists, we may have to accept that there are some things we simply cannot know. To make matters worse, there may be other factors operating which we do not know about. We repeat: even if we have carried out the most meticulous analysis in which we have allowed for all confounding factors that we can think of, it still remains a possibility that the really important factor remains hidden.

An interesting further example from a related field arose in a study of the effect of 'teaching style' on the performance of children in school.[6] The question was: is the traditional style, in which what happens in the classroom is highly structured, more conducive to good performance than a more relaxed and informal approach? A clear advantage to one or other would seem to indicate that one or other style should be adopted in all classrooms. However, there are many other factors at work whose effect might easily be overlooked, such as the age or experience of the teacher, for example.

As politicians and others know to their cost, the remedies they propose for social and economic ills often fail to work. Often, this may be due to the complex network of inter-connected factors being so confounded that it is almost impossible to know which one to change. The world is full of 'red herrings' and this is especially true in the world of intelligence testing.

Can we ever explain the black/white difference in IQ?

The fact that groups differ in average IQ is not, of itself, a source of great debate or division. The real bone of contention arises when it seems to point to differences in underlying mental ability. Does the black/white IQ difference in the United States, for example, indicate, in whole or part, a real difference originating in the genes or can it be wholly accounted for by environmental factors?[7] The foregoing discussion should have made it clear that, in strict logic, no definite answer can be given to that question. It will always remain a possibility that there is some environmental factor which is so confounded with race that it cannot be distinguished from it.

It was the discovery of this IQ difference between black and white, and Jensen's claim that it was plausible to attribute some of it, at least, to genetic differences, that sparked the furore following the publication of his article in the *Harvard Educational Review* in 1969. In order to resolve the uncertainty about how to interpret this difference it was, and *is*, necessary to do two things. First, to demonstrate whether the difference is really due to some environmental factor that is confounded with race. Secondly, to identify a relevant genetic difference between the groups, assuming one exists.

The possibility of confounding has given rise to an enormous amount of work. Often this is spoken of under the heading of test bias. A test is biased if it gives an advantage to one group rather than the other. In other words, we cannot be sure whether the score difference is due to ability to do the test or to environmental factors which affect the groups differently. This is often described in terms of cultural differences. As with the smoking and cancer example used above, one can never absolutely rule out environmental explanations of this kind. The best one can hope to do is to identify one possible explanation after another and then try to eliminate them one by one. The idea being that if we can eliminate all possible environmental factors, then what is left must be due to genetic factors. The trouble is that we can never be absolutely sure that we have got to the end of the list.

There are occasions where the very magnitude of a difference, as in this case, is such that it is scarcely credible that it could be wholly explained by environmental factors. It is argued that environmental factors certainly do have an effect on IQ but, where these have been thoroughly investigated, they rarely amount to more than enough to account for more than a few IQ points. Something else is needed to bridge the gap and innate ability is the obvious candidate. At this point in the discussion, common sense is likely to rear its head. Surely, the argument will go, any reasonable person would conclude that the odds seem heavily on a genetic explanation, given the difficulty of finding serious competitors on the environmental side. It certainly makes the genetic explanation more plausible but, adhering to strict logic, it must be allowed that an environmental explanation cannot be ruled out.

The plausibility derived from the dearth of environmental factors would be immensely strengthened if it were possible to identify, positively, some genetic contribution. This takes us back to g and the discussion about the lack of causal models for differences in intelligence. If g truly is a collective property of the brain, then it must reflect, to some degree at least, genetic endowment. Surely the problem is then easily solved by comparing the average g for the two groups. If we could show that the observed difference in IQ is indicative of a difference in g, the case would be made. After all, IQ was never anything better than second best. It is, as we have seen, a compromise measure influenced by several distinct dimensions of ability, whose value is also affected by environmental factors. From the start then, it was clear that, at best, it could not take us beyond mere plausibility. Why not go straight to g which is much closer to the genes? The reason should be obvious. As a latent variable it cannot be observed. Even if it could, g has an arbitrary scaling and so presents us with all the problems which we have met with IQ.

Lacking g, the obvious alternative is to use g-scores as the next best thing. This would still not side-step the scaling problems but, if the difference were large, these should not be crippling. However, there is another complication which we have glossed over so far. Whereas IQ is a sum of scores, g-scores are essentially weighted sums where the weights depend on the data. These, therefore, create problems for making comparisons.[8]

There is, however, a half-way house which has been investigated by Jensen, building on an idea from Spearman. Jensen calls it the *Spearman hypothesis.* His idea was to base the comparison on test items which are known to be relatively pure indicators of *g* rather on IQ itself. We saw in chapter 10 how items could be distinguished by the extent to which they reflected the value of *g*. They were said to load heavily on *g* or, even, to be saturated with *g*. If there are real genetic differences between black and white, they ought to be more apparent in the scores on items which are known to be particularly good indicators of *g*. These indicators are not perfect indicators of *g*, of course, but they are relatively uncontaminated. Raven's Matrices is a good example of a test item which appears to be such an indicator and the black/white difference does seem to be larger in this case. Jensen has analysed many data sets in this way with results supporting the Spearman hypothesis – that the purer the indicator, the bigger the difference. Within the wider psychometric community there continues to be a debate on whether the evidence does fully support the hypothesis.[9]

It is natural to wonder whether one could do better by using, not a single item, but an index based on several; their sum perhaps. This would give a better 'fix' on *g* and hence a firmer base for the conclusion. This does not appear to have been done.

Returning to the question of the title of this section, it may be that we will never be able to conclude, without a shadow of doubt, that the black/white difference is due, in part at least, to genetic factors. The evidence available makes it plausible, some would say convincing, but certainty eludes us.

The question then is: what should we do? This brings us into the realm of decision making. There is a difference between what one ought to believe on the basis of the evidence and what one ought to do in the light of the evidence. When action has to be taken it must, necessarily, be on the basis of inconclusive evidence. If we only acted on the basis of certainties, we would seldom do anything at all. Instead we take 'calculated risks'. What we are then doing, in effect, is to replace the empirical evidence, which we lack, by a judgement based on our total experience of the world. We are using what we can distil from the accumulated store of information in our heads to make up for what is missing. At its best, this is what common sense actually does. There is nothing wrong with doing this as long as we are clear that we have gone beyond the evidence. But in doing so we are moving out of the strictly scientific ambit and we must then recognise that differences of judgement are inevitable.

The crux of the problem is that ordinal level measures are not adequate to answer the questions we have posed. Until we have better, brain-based, measures of intelligence which measure, at a higher level, what *g* and IQ are supposed to reflect, it will be impossible to obtain conclusive evidence.

The question of group differences has also arisen in connection with the Flynn effect which refers to the increase in observed IQ over time. It seems unlikely that this increase, of about fifteen IQ points per generation, can have much to do with changes in innate ability, particularly if the latter is inherited. It also seems unlikely that the environmental effects can have produced such large differences in such a short time. This example differs from the black/white issue in that time is now an important element of the problem. This opens up further possibilities for understanding group differences by showing that interactions can play an important role, and that is covered in the next chapter.

12   Is intelligence inherited?

What is the argument about?

The inheritance of intelligence is one of the most hotly disputed topics in this field. The argument is not really about *whether* it is inherited; hardly anyone nowadays disputes that intelligence is, to some extent, handed down from parents to children. The real debate is about whether the contribution of inheritance to a person's intelligence is a major or a minor factor. It is sometimes claimed that as much as 80 per cent of intelligence is attributable to inheritance, while more modest claims put it between 40 and 60 per cent. Yet others, like Leon Kamin, have doubted whether there is any good evidence for the heritable component to be much above zero.[1] It is rare for anyone, it seems, to spend much time considering what these percentages actually measure and how relevant they are to the point at issue. That is the subject of the present chapter.

To begin with, we shall couch the discussion in terms of the generic term 'intelligence', since many of the points we wish to make are relevant whether we are talking about a g-score, IQ or any other similar index purporting to measure intelligence. Many writers are far from clear about what it is that is supposed to be inherited. A more precise discussion of heritability requires us to speak in terms of some particular measure of intelligence. Almost all of the research on the matter relates to IQ, so we shall revert to talking about IQ when we come to particulars. In one sense this is absurd, because a moment's thought will show that IQ cannot be inherited. It is genes that are inherited – the programme for constituting the individual. The real question is whether what is passed on to children leads to the offspring scoring similarly on intelligence tests to their parents. For practical purposes it is sufficient to work in terms of IQ.

It is easy to see why the battle should be contested so hotly on this particular ground when one considers the political and educational implications of giving priority to either extreme. The polarisation into nature or nurture – genes or the environment – has often been the battle ground for those whose zeal outruns their comprehension. Indeed, to be labelled a hereditarian is, in some quarters, to be guilty of the archetypal modern heresy. Questions of equal opportunity and discrimination are often debated without regard to the implied assumptions being made about heritability. If a person's intelligence is, essentially, a fixed quantity present from conception or birth and largely unaffected by environmental influences, there is little point in spending vast quantities of public money in an attempt to improve it. On the other hand, if nurture rather than nature is the dominant factor in determining intelligence, then it should be possible to increase a person's intelligence with obvious benefits both to the individual and society. Indeed, it would be a simple matter of social justice that this should be done. Those on the political left, who believe that society can be improved by changing its structure and organisation, have the ground cut from beneath them if it can be shown that there is very little that such changes can do. Those on the political right, who believe that sound political programmes need to be based on a recognition of 'the nature of the beast', have their aspirations blighted if it turns out that intelligence is not immutable.

Those coming new to the field must wonder what all the fuss is about. The common sense view would be that intelligence must be inherited, like almost everything else. Children resemble their parents in appearance and in so many ways that it is taken for granted that the explanation lies in the genes. The striking discoveries about the inheritance of conditions like haemophilia and schizophrenia are merely the tip of a very large iceberg. What is so special, newcomers might ask, about this mysterious thing called intelligence that distinguishes it from all other human attributes?

The responses which are typically made to this challenge are twofold. Taken in its most extreme form, it can be argued that intelligence is a fiction and therefore the question of its inheritance does not arise. The other, less extreme counter, allows that intelligence is inherited to some degree, but that its influence is swamped by a multitude of environmental factors. The apparent importance of inheritance then arises from its close link with the environment. Interestingly, the commonly accepted orthodoxy, in the United States at least, seems to have swung from a pro-inheritance to a pro-environment stance in the 1960s and 1970s without any matching shift in the weight of evidence! This curious phenomenon was explored by Snyderman and Robson[2] in their book on the IQ controversy. This is a fascinating and instructive account of the role of the media in the dissemination of information and the formation of public opinion on scientific matters.

The debate has been given a new impetus by the publicity surrounding the completion of the mapping of the human genome. It is claimed that we now have the book of instructions for constructing a human person. This has fostered the view that almost any human characteristic can be attributed to the genes. That, one must presume, includes the structure of the brain. If intelligence is determined, in part at least, by the brain, then it seems obvious that the inheritance will play a part in determining the individual's intelligence. However, it is equally clear that other factors also have an influence on almost all aspects of the person. Height, for example, may be mainly determined by the genes but we know that it can also be affected by nutrition and exercise in the early years. This poses the very tricky problem of trying to separate out the effects of heredity and environment. It is not even clear, at this stage, whether it can be done at all. The question of the chapter title sounds simple enough, but the quick-sands facing the intrepid explorer are treacherous and ubiquitous.

One thing, at least, should be made clear at the outset. To say that 45 per cent of a person's intelligence is attributable to inheritance does not mean what most people coming new to the field would expect it to mean! It invites us to think of intelligence as being a mixture made up of 45 parts from the parents and 55 parts from the environment. Each individual thus gets their due quota and that is the end of the matter. It is actually a statement, not about an individual, but about variation in a population, as we shall see. In fact, it is yet another example of a collective property.

Some rudimentary genetics

It is much easier to investigate the heritability of traits dependent on a single gene, like premature baldness in males, which you either have or you do not have. This is an 'all or nothing' thing and there is a direct link between the gene the individual has (the genotype) and the physical characteristic (the phenotype) which depends on it. The number of cases in successive generations can be counted and one can ask whether or not the proportions match those predicted by genetic theory. The classical example concerns Mendel's peas. Mendel conducted experiments by crossing round peas with wrinkled peas and then observed the proportions in which the two kinds of pea appeared among the offspring. He discovered simple laws, named after him, which predict how 'roundness' and 'wrinkledness' are inherited.

When dealing with the inheritance of something like intelligence, which varies continuously (we have assumed!), we have a much more complicated situation. To see what is at issue let us start with a less contentious example. Consider, yet again, human height. This is not an 'all or nothing' characteristic, so it cannot be determined by a single gene. Instead, it seems more reasonable to suppose that the height of a person is influenced by many genes each making a modest contribution to the final figure. The height of an offspring will therefore depend on which particular selection of genes is inherited – half from one parent and half from the other. If we have a tall father and a tall mother, we might expect the height of the offspring to be tall, since all of the relevant genes will have come from tall parents. If one parent is tall and the other short, we might expect the offspring to fall somewhere between the two, since about half the genes relevant to height determination will have come from the parent who has 'tall' genes and the other half from the other parent who has 'short' genes.

It is important to add, for later reference, that the effects of the genes do not always simply add up in this way. The effect of any particular gene may depend on which other genes are present.

As we have already noted, environmental factors will also play their part and, as we shall see, these may modify the effect of the genes. In judging the relative importance of inheritance and environment, we shall then have to find some way of separating the two effects. The study of the inheritance of continuous variables is known as biometrical genetics and the major early figure in this field was Sir Ronald Fisher.[3] He invented the measure known as *heritability*, which was designed to separate out and quantify the effects of nature and nurture. A statistical account of these matters will be found in Sham Pak 1998.

Heritability

Heritability is expressed on a percentage scale and it purports to tell us how much of *the variation in a population* can be accounted for by inheritance and how much by environment. The measurement of heredity is actually quite a sophisticated idea. Before we plunge in, it may help to approach the general question from first principles, starting from the fact that children often do resemble their parents in matters of intelligence. Could we not simply look at the correlation between the IQs of parents and their children? We could, and we would, find a positive correlation. Does it not follow then that some, at least, of the children's ability must have come from their parents? Not necessarily, because environmental factors are also involved. Intelligent parents are likely to provide an intellectually stimulating environment for their offspring and it may be that fact, rather than the genetic link, which accounts for the correlation. Trying a different tack, our imaginary interlocutor might point out that children in the same family often seem to be similar in intelligence. There are variations, of course, but variation within families often seems much less than that between families. This is, surely, just what we would expect from the common genetic input which individuals with the same parents share. Indeed it is, but they also shared a similar pre-natal environment in their mother's womb and, very frequently, a very similar upbringing. Cousins and other relations, with some common ancestry would also be expected to show some correlation in IQ but, again, this cannot easily be distinguished from the common environmental influences. In the technical language used in the last chapter, the effects of heredity and environment are said to be *confounded*.

The only hope, it would seem, of disentangling the effects of inheritance and environment is to find some means of eliminating one or the other altogether and seeing what effect the one remaining had. Fortunately this is sometimes done for us, approximately at least, by nature. Identical twins have the same genetic inheritance and hence any difference in their intelligence must be attributable to environmental influences. If the differences between the IQs of pairs of identical twins are much the same as between unrelated children, then we may infer that heredity is contributing very little. Knowing that two children have a common genetic background would then tell us nothing about the similarity of their IQs. On the other hand, if identical twins had IQs which were generally much closer than would be the case with unrelated children, that fact would be a pointer to the presence of a common genetic influence.

Twin comparisons have been the backbone of investigations into the heritability of IQ. More detailed comparisons are possible. Identical twins, known as monozygotic twins (because they come from a single egg), can be compared with dizygotic twins (from separate eggs). The former have all their genes in common, whereas the latter have only half in common, just like any other siblings. More distant relatives have lesser, but known proportions in common. Such comparisons lead to a hierarchy of expected correlations based on the proportion of common genetic material. The more genes two individuals have in common, the higher one would expect the correlation between their IQs to be – if inheritance plays any part.

Eliminating environmental effects is also possible, though more difficult in practice. To make such a comparison we need to identify individuals who have shared the same environment but have different inheritance. Adopted children are obvious candidates for such comparisons. Their IQs can be compared with the natural offspring of the parents of the families into which they are adopted, or with the IQs of their adoptive parents and their biological parents. If there is a genetic component, one would expect children to be closer to their biological parents in IQ than their adoptive parents. But such comparisons can be vitiated by the practice of some adoption agencies of trying to match the abilities of the children with those of prospective parents. There are many other complications which make the inferences based on such comparisons less secure than they might appear. For example, the parental expectations, and possibly, the resources devoted to adopted children may be different from those of natural children. Again, children brought up in the same family do not experience exactly the same environment. The first child is brought up alone until the second arrives and so the second has the experience of having an elder sibling, which is something the first can never have. Nevertheless, the more common environmental factors that two individuals have in common, the higher one would expect the correlation between their IQs to be – if environment plays any part at all.

Unfortunately, the distinctions are not always as clear-cut as we would wish. Almost any comparisons which we think of making will, almost inevitably, leave a loophole for the most determined critic and we may despair of ever being able to make fully valid comparisons. Nevertheless, there have been many thousands of empirical studies in this area and it is difficult to avoid the general conclusion which emerges from them. In spite of the individual blemishes which one can

Table 12.1 *Estimated correlations between IQs of the relatives stated under two environmental conditions: raised together (T), raised apart (A).*

Relationship	Environment	Correlation
Twins (monozygotic)	T	0.85
Twins (monozygotic)	A	0.74
Twins (dizygotic)	T	0.59
Siblings	T	0.46
Siblings	A	0.24
Midparent/child	T	0.50
Single parent/child	T	0.41
Single parent/child	A	0.24
Adoptive parent/child	T	0.20

find in almost all studies, their cumulative effect is impressive. In order to give some idea of typical results, we quote some correlations from *Intelligence, Genes and Success: Scientists Respond to the Bell Curve*.[4] This has the merit of being as near to an independent assessment of the evidence as one is likely to find. The figures given in table 3.1 of chapter 3 of that book are a summarisation of 212 correlations. Some results, extracted from that table, are reproduced in table 12.1.

These correlations are derived from many studies and are estimated using a model of how the various effects combine. The model is well supported by the data (see Devlin *et al.* 1997). The correlations are listed systematically according to the degree of relationship and, with the exception of siblings, in decreasing order of expected value. 'Expected' here means 'on the basis of the known genetic material the pairs have in common and on how the various factors are assumed to interact'. Thus monozygotic twins reared together have all of their genes in common and most of their environment; siblings raised apart have less in common than those reared together and so on. The fact that the first correlation is only 0.85 and not 1 implies that being raised together does not guarantee an identical IQ. There must be sufficient variation in the upbringing environment to cause the observed difference. (We must not forget that IQ is not a precise measure but subject to all the uncertainties of the measuring situation.) On this evidence one can be confident that inheritance plays some part in determining IQ. The question now is: can we go further and quantify the contribution made by the genes?

How can we measure heritability?

We have emphasised that there is no way we can say how much of a particular individual's intelligence can be attributed to inheritance and how much to environment. The only kind of statement which we can validly make relates to a population and this, as we shall see, places important restrictions on what we can say.

In any population, IQ is usually scaled to have a pre-determined value for its variation (measured by the standard deviation or variance) and so calculating this value is not necessary. Nevertheless, it will make the rationale easier to understand if we imagine starting by calculating this variation from first principles. In any population we can, in principle, measure the IQ of every member. Although we cannot split an individual's IQ into two parts, such that one can be linked with the genes and the other with the environment, we *can*, in certain circumstances, and in a certain sense, make such a decomposition for the population as a whole. The way to do this is to work in terms of the variability of IQ as measured by a *sum of squares*.

We start with the sum of squares of all the IQs in the population. This is calculated in the following way. First subtract the average IQ from each individual score, then square the result and add up the squared differences. The resulting 'sum of squares' measures the variability of IQ in the population; the more widely scattered the scores, the larger the sum of squares. The reason for choosing the sum of squares is that it allows us to divide it into parts, each of which can be identified with a different source of variation in which we are interested – heredity and environment, in this case. This was a particular insight of Fisher, who then showed that a sensible measure of heritability could be found by decomposing the sum of squares in this fashion. However, thus far we have no indication how this decomposition takes place and what it signifies. We therefore need to spend a little time exploring why this approach works.

As so often, we have to start by behaving as though we knew more than we actually do. Let us go back to the point where we noted that there was no basis for splitting an individual IQ into two parts. That does not prevent us from imagining that an IQ is, nevertheless, made up of two contributions – one from the parents and one from the environment. If that were the case, we might wonder what would happen to the two parts in the process of differencing, squaring and adding up which we have just described. The answer is that we would get just the same answer as if we had started with the two separate components, computed their sums of squares and then added *them* up. This is what is meant by saying that the sum of squares for the population can be decomposed into two parts each depending on a different source of variation.

However, the position is a little more complicated than that because there are two parents each making a contribution to the genetic make-up of the offspring. There will thus be two genetic components to be considered. The main further complication arises because the two parental contributions do not necessarily 'add up'. A moment ago we suggested that a tall father and a tall mother might be expected to have a tall child, whereas a short father and tall mother might have a child of middling height, which is what we would expect if the parental contributions added up. That is, if the offspring's characteristic was derived in equal proportions from each parent. This does not always happen. Sometimes there is an *interaction*, which means that the effect which one contribution has depends on the magnitude of the other. This might mean, for example, that some of the contributing genes from one parent might have their effects modified by which genes happen to be present from the other parent. The genetic contribution to the IQ of the offspring can thus be divided into two parts: the *additive* part, which is what would have been present if there were no interaction, and the *interaction*, which accounts for the remainder.

The total variation in the population thus has contributions from three sources: the additive genetic component, the genetic interaction component and the environmental component. The remarkable thing, on which Fisher's idea for measuring heritability depends, is that the total sum of squares can be decomposed into three parts such that each depends on only one source of variation. Thus:

Total variation = Additive genetic variation + Interaction genetic variation + Environmental variation.

This goes one step beyond the simple decomposition we envisaged at the outset by splitting the genetic sum of squares into the two parts just identified. A more detailed analysis would require us to make further subdivisions but these are sufficient to make the main points.

From this equation we can begin to see how heritability might be measured. If the environmental contribution is the major part, the last term on the right will account for most of the total variation. If the effect of the genes is dominant, it will be the first two terms that play the main part. An obvious way of measuring the genetic contribution is then to express the genetic variation as a proportion – or percentage – of the total variation. This was what Fisher suggested. Thus:

Heritability = Genetic variation/Total variation.

Does this not ignore the distinction we have just drawn between the two parts of the genetic variation? It does, and we get two versions of the index according to how we decide to take account of the two parts. This choice is important because the one used in biological applications is smaller than the one used by psychometricians. When figures of heritability are being bandied about in debates on the heritability of IQ, it is important to know which version is being used. Biologists favour what is called the narrow definition, where the genetic contribution is measured only by the additive component. This is because it is the more relevant quantity for their applications. They are mainly concerned with plant or animal breeding, where they wish to predict the effect of different matings. Since there is usually no way of knowing which particular genes are involved, from either parent, there is no way of predicting what the interactions might be and, hence, their effects. The additive part of the genetic contribution is therefore the 'predictable' part of the variation. The part arising from the interactions is not predictable because we do not know which other genes there are to interact with.

Psychometricians, on the other hand, use the broad version of the index in which both the additive and 'interaction' parts are included, because they are more interested in describing the total effect of the genetic contribution. In other words, in showing how much of the total variation in the population would be removed if the genetic effect were not present. Herrnstein and Murray make considerable use of the broad version of the index, though they do not distinguish it from the narrow version.[5]

How can we estimate heritability?

There is one rather obvious gap in our treatment so far. How can we actually estimate the index in practice? There is no problem about the total variation. We simply measure the IQs of the members of the population – or, more likely, a representative sample of them – and calculate their sum of squares. To estimate either of the other components we somehow have to find circumstances where we already know one of the components. Identical twins have an identical genetic inheritance. For this reason, any variation in their IQ must be attributable to environmental factors. Hence we can, in principle, make some estimate of the environmental effect in their case. Similarly step-children, cousins, grandparents and grandchildren and other relations have known proportions of their genes in common. On the other side, adopted children with different genetic inheritance, but brought up in the same family, are subject to much less environmental variation than similar children reared apart. If, in one way or another, we can combine all these pieces of information, and make some estimate of the environmental variation, we can get the genetic contribution needed for the broad version of the index by subtraction from the total. Fortunately, this is possible.

The index of heritability depends on the population

As we noted earlier, Fisher's index is specific to a particular population. This means that its value depends on how much environmental variation there actually is in the population. If, for example, we had a population which was environmentally homogeneous, the contribution of the environment to the variation in IQ would necessarily be small, and hence the proportion attributable to the genes would be correspondingly high. Conversely, as the environment becomes more variable, the heritability index will diminish. This prevents us from making any absolute statements about the relative importance of the two contributions to the variability. The index only makes sense with respect to a particular population at a particular time. Suppose, for example, that steps were taken to reduce environmental variation. This might be done, for example, by equalising opportunities for access to education, providing food supplements for children from poor families and so on. Reducing the environmental component of the total sum of squares in this way would inevitably increase the heritability as measured by Fisher's index whereas, in reality, what was inherited would not have changed. It would, however, be less diluted by environmental factors and so appear to be a more dominant part of the variability of IQ.

This all leads to an apparently paradoxical situation. Suppose that some source of environmental variation had been identified which had a marked effect on IQ. If action were taken to increase the IQs of those at the lower end of the distribution by changing the environmental influences, this would reduce the environmental variation of that factor. Other things being unchanged, this would increase the coefficient of heritability without affecting the process of inheritance itself! The measure of heritability is thus extremely limited. It measures only the *relative* contributions of the two main sources of variation in a particular population. Comparisons between populations are not legitimate.

In practice things are very much more complicated. The environmental influences can be subdivided in many ways. One important division is between the environmental effects in the womb before birth and those afterwards. A second is that between the family environment, which siblings share, and the external environment. To separate out these and other components requires large amounts of good quality data and expert statistical resources for modelling and estimation. The mere mention of these should instil a sense of the high degree of uncertainty to be attached to statements about heritability.[6] Before we can profitably pursue these matters we need to digress to clarify what is involved in disentangling a complex web of contributing factors.

Confounding, covariation and interaction

We have already met 'confounding' in chapter 11 in the context of comparing two groups. If, for example, we were comparing two ethnic groups who also happened to differ totally in respect of educational background, then we would not be able to tell whether any difference between the groups was due to ethnicity or education. Confounding in a case like this amounts to a complete mixing up of the two factors and there is no way of separating them without more information.

In many situations the confounding may not be total. If, in the previous example, there was some variation in education within each ethnic group, it would be possible to extract some information about the effect of education when ethnicity was held constant. The differing effects of education could then be seen within each ethnic group, to some degree. The term *covariation* is used to describe the situation when two factors have some degree of association. This means that the effect of one factor will partly hide the effect of the other.

Covariation arises when considering the joint effect of genes and environment on IQ. Although the two are unlikely to be totally confounded, they do often co-vary. Environment is a many-faceted thing. Intelligent parents are likely to have relatively high incomes which will enable them to provide a stimulating environment for their children. Those children are already better endowed genetically and the effect that one factor has on IQ partly obscures the effect of the other. Both will make their contribution but it will be impossible to attribute their overall effect unambiguously to one source or the other. A partial separation may be possible because, at any level of environmental influence, there will be some variation in the influence of the genes.

Confounding and covariation pose problems enough, but worse is to come. We need to look more closely at interaction. We have already mentioned possible interactions between the effects of the genes but the concept is of much wider significance. In the case of confounding, we cannot properly perceive what the factors are doing because they get in one another's way, so to speak. It may be, however, that the effect of any one factor is influenced by what other factors are present and to what degree. When that happens we have said that they *interact*. Interactions are extremely common. One of the most familiar examples is that which sometimes occurs between alcohol and a drug. Either, taken by itself may, for example, impair driving ability. But when alcohol and some drugs are taken together, the effect may be much more serious than would be expected by adding their separate effects. This might be due to a chemical reaction in the stomach in which a new and much more potent chemical is formed. Or it might be that one drug creates conditions in which the other has a broader scope for action.

Interactions do not necessarily result in an enhanced effect. One factor may inhibit the effect of the other. This is the intention, if not always the effect, of the various remedies proposed for countering the effect of excessive alcohol consumption. Many simple remedies for common complaints, like indigestion, are examples involving interactions. An anti-acid tablet will mitigate the effect of foods which stimulate the release of acid in the stomach by neutralising its effect. The possibility of interactions must always be borne in mind because their presence makes it impossible to describe the effects of a factor in a simple way. Because it is so important to grasp the idea, we shall give a further example which, again, has nothing to do with intelligence.[7]

The uptake of carbon dioxide by trees, through the leaves, is an important subject of research because it has implications for atmospheric pollution. One might hope that the extra carbon dioxide discharged into the atmosphere by human activity would be soaked up by trees. However, it turns out that this may not always be the case, because an increase in carbon dioxide emission is often accompanied by an increase in the release of sulphur dioxide. This is also absorbed by leaves and this happens in such a way that the pathways for the absorption of carbon dioxide are blocked. The absorption of rising levels of atmospheric carbon dioxide is thus inhibited by the parallel process for sulphur dioxide. The two processes interact. Calculations of the potential for reducing the level of carbon dioxide in the atmosphere which ignored the amount of sulphur dioxide present would over-estimate the potential absorption.

Exactly the same kind of problem arises when studying the determinants of IQ. We have already noted that the effect of one gene often depends on which other genes are present. It is also the case that the effect of a gene may depend on the environment in which it finds itself. This means that the independence required by the index of heritability between inheritance and environment does not occur in practice. One cannot say, therefore, that a particular gene, or combination of genes, will have such and such an effect because that will depend upon the environmental circumstances in which it, or they, are brought into play. The effects of the genes and the environment therefore come as a package and their combined effect depends on the particular mix of items in the package.

In principle, and given sufficient data, it might be possible to decompose the total variation into further components, each associated with different sources of variation. However, the more we do this, the less sensible it is to try to summarise this extra information in a single index of heritability. Some of the subtlety will, inevitably, be lost. Complicated questions do not always admit of simple answers. The short answer to the question: how important are the genes in determining IQ? is: it all depends . . .

An important part of the environment is composed of other persons with whom an individual interacts. Parents, and others, will react differently to a lively outgoing inquisitive child than to a withdrawn placid child. The child, for its part, will favour environments in which it feels comfortable. To an extent, therefore, the child creates its own environment by seeking out, or stimulating others to provide, an environment in which its own genetically determined characteristics best fit. Is the child's revealed intelligence then due to environment or heredity? There is certainly a correlation between the kind of environment in which the child operates and its genetic endowment, but how far is it proper to attribute the outcome of their joint effect to one or the other? The environment depends on the genetic endowment. Should it, therefore, be classified as part of the genetic contribution or as part of the environmental contribution? The problem here is that there is no clear dividing line between heredity and environment – one person's inheritance is another person's environment! The attempt to measure, in any precise sense, how much of a person's mental ability is inherited and how much is acquired is thus doomed from the start.

To conclude this section, we give another example of a way in which the question of heritability may be more subtle than first appears. It can happen that intelligence is indirectly affected by the inheritance of something quite different. For example, Deary 2000 (p. 26) mentions the inherited metabolic disorder known as phenylketonuria (PKN). This involves an inability to break down the essential amino acid, phenylalanine and one of its effects, if untreated, is to produce mental retardation. It is known that this disorder is the result of the offspring receiving the relevant recessive trait from each parent. The low IQ of the child in this case is inherited by the mechanism just described but it has nothing to do with the intelligence of the parents. In general, what is inherited comes as a package and it could happen that the elements of that package interact with one another, the effects possibly being delayed. It is important that these things should be kept in proportion. PKN, and other related conditions, affects something between 1 in 20,000 and 1 in 30,000 of Caucasian and Oriental births. The incidence of similar effects would have to be much higher before they seriously distorted the picture.

Just how far interactions might interfere with the 'obvious' interpretations of the differences and correlations which we uncover can be seen by returning to the celebrated case of the Flynn effect.

The Flynn effect re-visited

In the last chapter we noted the extraordinary increase in IQ which appears to have taken place in the last few decades in many parts of the world. Roughly speaking this amounts to about fifteen IQ points per generation. This means that the typical person, whose IQ was in the middle of the range a generation ago, would find themselves much lower in today's distribution. At first sight one might see this as very strong empirical evidence for the determination of IQ by environmental factors because it is difficult to see what biological factors could do so much in so little time. Equally however, and given our empirical knowledge of the modest effects that environmental factors typically have, it is not easy to imagine what environmental factors could produce such a big change in such a relatively short time. Whatever has happened cannot reasonably be attributed to the additive effects of heredity and environment. Something much more fundamental must have been going on.

First thoughts can be very misleading and this is the case here. One possible explanation depends on remembering that IQ is not g but only an indicator of it. The fact that IQ changes does not logically require g to have changed. It may simply be the relationship between them that has changed. All sorts of other ingenious suggestions have been made in a similar vein but these may all be on the wrong track. Alternatively, it could be the result of interaction effects which is why we have raised the matter again at this juncture. This explanation has been suggested by Flynn himself, in collaboration with Dickens,[8] and it serves to illustrate just how potent interactions can be over time.

The prime purpose of Dickens and Flynn's paper was to resolve what, to current thinking, has appeared as a paradox. On the one hand it is widely accepted that a substantial part of IQ is inherited and yet, on the other, large increases have taken place which must be due to environmental sources. The claim in the subtitle 'The IQ paradox resolved' is, perhaps, an overstatement. What their paper clearly demonstrates is that interactions between hereditary and environmental factors can produce surprising effects. Furthermore, they could produce just the kind of effect observed in the paradox and also provide explanations of several other curious observations. The latter include the fact that the environmental contribution to IQ seems to decline with age, whereas one might have expected the opposite.

Some of the potential consequences of interactions in this field have been known for some time, and a few have been mentioned already, but Dickens and Flynn have synthesised them and spelt out their implications in quantitative terms. Here we shall only be able to indicate in the broadest of terms how their thinking goes.

The first model, which they describe as 'matching and mixing environmental effects', supposes that the environmental effects are partly determined by inheritance as we envisaged above. There we imagined a child seeking out congenial environments for the exercise of his or her natural talents. Introducing this matching of environment and genes has the effect of masking some of the contribution of the environment and so makes the genes look more influential than they actually are.

The second model shows that the matching of genes and environment can act as a multiplier of environmental effects. This means that quite small variations in genetic endowment can, in the course of time, produce large changes in IQ through the magnifying effect of the environment. This remarkable effect depends on the matching taking place in a particular fashion. This time it is IQ which is supposed to find a matching environment. Initially, the authors suppose, IQ depends only on inheritance but then inheritance has its effect on the environment which, in its turn, further enhances IQ. That will lead to the seeking out of yet more stimulating environments leading, by the same cycle of events, to yet further increases in IQ.

The third model recognises the fact, pointed out above, that the environment is partly composed of other people. Their IQs will have been influenced by their own genetic endowment and past environment but they, being part of the current environment, will have an impact on current IQs. There is thus a social multiplier effect tending to increase general IQ levels over time.

In order to illustrate the idea behind what is a highly technical argument, Dickens and Flynn use the case of the shift in interest from baseball to basketball in the United States and the enormous increase in basketball skills. There is a close parallel with the growth of interest in snooker, notably in the UK. The skills on which success depends may well be inherited to some extent, but it is their interaction with environmental factors which plays havoc with the attempt to apportion responsibility between nature and nurture. A small inherited advantage may lead parents to provide equipment and opportunities for coaching for the budding snooker player which will probably lead to improved skills. This effects a degree of matching of genes and environment. The improved skills may then lead to selection to play at a higher level; this will bring more competition and even better coaching and facilities. This marks the beginning of the multiplier effect in which a small initial advantage is amplified into a much bigger one.

Finally, there is the social multiplier in which television is a potent factor. The action in snooker, like basketball, fits neatly into a television screen. As the general quality of play rises, exposure on television is likely to increase, and with it the perceived standard to which newcomers must aspire rises also. The generally higher standard of play now becomes an environmental influence conducive to yet higher levels of play, and so on.

All of this may sound rather speculative, both in relation to snooker and basketball and to the escalating levels of IQ with which we began. To test the details of the theory empirically would be very difficult but some of its broad predictions can be checked. Such an exercise shows that models of this kind do predict much larger changes in IQ than either genes or environment could plausibly produce if acting independently. For our present purposes, it shows that the simple model, on which the traditional measure of hereditability is based, is not adequate. All such measures therefore need to be treated with great caution.

The heritability of g

In conclusion, we return to the distinction we have made between IQ and g. Hitherto we have been talking about the heritability of IQ, because this is the thing that is most often measured and with which the literature is primarily concerned. The complications which have been exercising us arise mainly from the fact that IQ is partly determined by environmental factors. If we could get behind IQ and focus on g, things might be much simpler. If, as we have speculated earlier, g is also a measure of brain structure and performance, we might expect it to be much less affected by environmental factors, for the simple reason that its value should be fixed much earlier in life. There is no way we can directly examine the heritability of g because it is a latent variable. We do, however, have access to g-scores which are estimates of what an individual's g would be if it were scaled to have a standard normal distribution.

However, a little reflection reveals something slightly odd about doing this. If *g* really is a measure of some innate property of the brain, determined by or shortly after birth, there will not have been very much opportunity for environmental factors, apart from pre-natal influences, to introduce a significant amount of variation in the way it performs. In consequence the *proportion* of variation attributable to the genes in the broad sense will, necessarily, be rather large. We seem to have come perilously close to a tautology: if *g* were defined as something which is primarily a property of the brain fixed very early in life, it must, necessarily, be highly heritable. In a sense, therefore, it is rather pointless to talk about the heritability of *g* because that is virtually implied by this definition of heritability!

An entirely different approach would be to look directly at the influence of the genes on brain structure. If it turned out that those areas of the brain chiefly involved in the verbal and spatial activities, which come into play in intelligence tests, were genetically determined, then one would expect to find similar performance from those sharing the same genes. In short, if the hardware of brains is inherited, then the performance that goes with that hardware should be inherited also. The debate would then switch from a discussion of the meaning of statistical correlations to the less contentious realm of the inheritance of bodily characteristics. Some research in this direction has already been carried out.[9] This compared the brain structure (determined by MRI scans) of identical twins and of fraternal twins and it showed that the more genes twins had in common the greater the similarity in the relevant parts of their brains. These correlations were reflected in their performance in tasks of the kind used in IQ tests. This work is of a preliminary nature, and the number of cases was very small, but it indicates the direction in which one should look to take the debate further.

This seems to be an appropriate place to leave the reader to reflect on the subtleties of the nature of intelligence and the degree of confusion which remains to be cleared up. In the final chapter we turn to an assessment of the current state of play.

13   Facts and fallacies

Terminology

The debates on intelligence have been long and fierce. It sometimes seems that the longer they continue the farther we get from any resolution. Some objections, like many of those aired in the wake of the publication of *The Bell Curve*, were little more than the predictable rantings of those whose ideological toes had been trodden on, but others are more serious and need to be addressed. Early objections were raised to IQ measures on the grounds that extraneous and irrelevant factors like fatigue and 'training' could distort the measure. Such problems are more to do with bias and reliability and can, to some extent, be controlled. Much more serious are those that challenge the very foundations of the enterprise. Often these objections are expressed by questioning the truth of statements which have wide currency, and seem to be taken for granted by the advocates of intelligence testing. In coming to the end of our journey we must attempt to separate the facts from the fallacies.[1]

A convenient way to do this is to focus, principally, on two writers who have obligingly drawn attention to the rocks on which they think the good ship founders. First among these is Gould, who repeatedly claimed that intelligence is not a *single*, *innate*, *heritable* and *measurable* '*thing*'. This runs like a refrain through *The Mismeasure of Man* and its five elements cover most of the significant objections that have been raised to intelligence testing. A second useful point of reference is Howe's *12 'facts' about intelligence which are not true*. These are less precisely expressed but they are also worth considering.

Before we can resolve the conflicts, it is essential to be clear about terminology. It really matters whether we are talking about intelligence, IQ or *g*. In fact, getting this simple point clear is sufficient to resolve many of the confusions which be-devil the debate. At the risk of boring the reader, we must, therefore, repeat once more the distinctions between the three main terms.

Intelligence This is the term used in ordinary discourse to refer to mental (or cognitive) ability. We all use it and have a general idea of what we mean by it, but its meaning is too imprecise to be useful for a scientific treatment of the subject. It has been used in this book only in this generic sense.

The Intelligence Quotient This is an index calculated from the scores obtained on a set of test items which are judged by experts to encompass the abilities covered by the term 'intelligence'. It is not a fixed characteristic of the individual tested but will vary according to the particular set of items used, the circumstances under which the test is taken and so forth. We have distinguished between IQ as a prescription for calculating a measure, and the number which results from the calculation.

g This is a hypothetical construct introduced to explain the pattern of responses obtained in IQ, and similar, tests. Such patterns are typically consistent with the hypothesis that there is a *major* single dimension of variation in human mental abilities. Variation along this dimension corresponds quite closely to our intuitive notion of intelligence. It is, therefore, common to refer to *g* as general cognitive ability or, more simply, as general intelligence.

We have also suggested that *g* may describe a single major dimension of brain function or structure. If so, it could refer either to the brain at birth, or at some later point when development has effectively ceased.

Principal conclusions about IQ and *g*

As a point of reference for our subsequent evaluation of Gould's and Howe's criticisms, we state the position which we have arrived at on IQ and *g*. In essence, the position can be summarised, non-technically, as follows.

It is possible to construct indices, such as IQ, which correspond fairly closely to what in common parlance we mean by intelligence. The picture such indices convey is obscured by many extraneous factors which are not always easy to identify or control.

IQ is a measure which expresses an individual's position relative to others in the same population – and no more. Its scale of measurement has no natural origin or unit of measurement and the form of its distribution is a matter of convention. The only comparisons which it is valid to make are, therefore, those which do not depend upon these arbitrary features.

Apart from this, the main drawback of IQ is that it measures an amalgam of different kinds of 'intelligence'. Different IQ tests may mix these different kinds in varying proportions. This further undermines the possibility of valid comparisons, even within the same population, where different tests may have been used. This feature can be summarised by saying that IQ is trying to measure a multidimensional quantity.

The nature of this multidimensionality can be explored by factor analysis. This identifies a single major dimension of variation which is known as *g*, and this appears to correspond closely to what we understand by 'general cognitive ability'. However, *g* cannot be observed directly and its origin, spread and the form of its distribution are not determined by the data. We therefore have to make do with an 'estimate', the so-called g-score. A g-score is an index rather like IQ. It is, primarily, the one-dimensional character of g which makes it superior to IQ.

Both IQ and g, therefore, provide only a weak form of measurement. The basic reason for this is that the test scores, on which they depend, are only indirect indicators of what is going on in the brain, which must be the true seat of intelligence. Further progress depends upon being able to make more direct measures of relevant brain processes and structures.

Gould's five points[2]

We now examine how Gould's five points stand up to scrutiny in the light of our analysis. Gould claims that the following statements about intelligence are false.

(i)   Intelligence is a 'thing'[3]

Regarding intelligence as a 'thing' is known as the error of reification, or that of treating something as real that does not exist. Whether or not this is true depends on what you mean by a 'thing'. Intelligence is certainly not a 'thing' in the sense of being made of atoms which can be seen, smelled, touched, weighed or tasted. Neither are many other useful concepts, like the cost of living, or a symphony. Without getting too deeply into philosophical waters, we might pause to consider whether, or in what sense, Schubert's Unfinished Symphony is a 'thing'. There are many copies of the score; there are many physical representations of that score on discs and tapes from which sounds, recognisable as the symphony, can be re-created. There are memories in the brains of many people, but none of these things is a single entity which could be described as *the* symphony. Yet the symphony exists in the real sense that it can be recognised by people and, in consequence, influence their thoughts and actions. The effect which it has on a person may, in some circumstances, also be said to explain why they think or do something. It would, therefore, seem perverse to insist that it does not exist in some significant sense.

This reflection suggests that asking whether intelligence is a thing is not very helpful. A more relevant question is: is it a recognisable entity which can produce changes in the physical world that we can detect with our senses? Even if g, for example, is no more than a collective property of a set of test scores, then it certainly produces changes and imputing them to g is simply a way of speaking of them collectively. Collective properties *exist* by virtue of the existence of the individual entities which make up the collective. If, on the other hand, g also measures a property of the brain, then the things that happen in brains unquestionably produce changes in the body and, hence, in the wider world. On either count g is real.

Another way of approaching the question of reification, touched on above, is to ask whether the concept of intelligence *explains* things that happen in the world. In other words, are there things which happen which can be attributed to variations in what is commonly understood by the term intelligence? As we have seen, this is not such a simple question as it appears but, even if much of the evidence were to be discounted, ample remains to substantiate the claim. The intelligence of millions of people has been measured, more or less adequately, and hardly anyone disputes that the variation revealed corresponds, at least roughly, to ability. Countless decisions have been made on the basis of the differences revealed which have affected individual careers, for example.

The charge of reification is, therefore, irrelevant to the main issue. What matters is whether or not a reasonably stable value can be ascertained for any individual which has predictive value. This is the case with IQ and also for *g*. Within their limits IQ and *g* are real in the pragmatic sense that they have predictive or explanatory value.

(ii) *Intelligence can be captured in a single number*

This is certainly not true for 'intelligence' in the general sense. It has been clearly demonstrated by factor analysis that more than one dimension is required to fix an individual's position in the space of mental ability

The IQ score *is* a single number which attempts to summarise an individual's ability, but factor analysis shows that it cannot fully summarise what is contained in the notion of intelligence. *g* is also a single (but unobservable) 'number' which corresponds to the major dimension of intelligence. It defines a universal fundamental ability, which is most useful in characterising a person's mental equipment.

Gould was, therefore, correct if he was thinking of IQ and wrong if he was thinking about *g*.

(iii) *Intelligence is measurable*

The term 'measurable' is ambiguous. If it means that individuals can be assigned unique places on a one-dimensional scale, then, as we have just seen, intelligence, being multidimensional, cannot be so measured. *g* is not measurable in that sense either. However, it is measurable in the weaker sense that individuals can be ranked on a one-dimensional scale. In other words, it provides a measure at the ordinal level. Gould's claim is not precise enough to be accepted or refuted, but we have described the position by saying that *g* is *weakly measurable*.

Turning to IQ, and thinking of it as a measuring instrument, as we must in this context, it is not strictly meaningful to speak of measuring IQ. It makes no more sense than to speak of measuring the length of a ruler or the duration of a clock.

(iv)   *Intelligence is innate*

This presumably means that intelligence is built into the physical structure of the body/brain by the genes and, therefore, cannot be altered by the environment (except, perhaps, by radical surgery!). IQ is certainly not innate in this sense. We have already noted that IQ scores can be changed, to some extent, by such things as special training, practice in taking IQ tests and enhancing the environment in various ways. g, on the other hand, results from an attempt to get beneath the surface of things to some more fundamental characteristic of the individual which influences (but does not precisely determine) such things as IQ. The belief that there is such a quantity is well supported by the empirical evidence. If, as we have conjectured, this quantity is also a reflection of the structure/functioning of the fully developed brain, g could be said to be innate in much the same way as eye colour or exceptional musical talent. A final judgement on this claim must await further research on the biological basis of intelligence but present indications do not support Gould.

(v)   *Intelligence is heritable*

It is almost certainly true that there is a heritable component in intelligence, whether we focus on IQ or g. The complexities are such that it is virtually impossible to disentangle the effects of the interactions between the genetic effects and the environmental factors. If heritability is measured by the proportion of variance in a population which is determined by the genes, estimates, made on various simplifying assumptions, put the figure anywhere between 40 and 80 per cent. It is thus impossible validly to claim a figure close to 100 per cent, which is what a strict biological determinism requires. Equally, any attempt to argue for a figure close to 0 per cent, as Lewontin did, will not stand close statistical scrutiny. Most of the current empirical evidence is strongly against Gould.

Similar points made by others

To Gould's list we may add two other claims which appear from time to time.

(vi)   *Intelligence is normally distributed*

This claim, referred to by King[4] among others, is both imprecise and certainly without foundation. If g is being referred to, it is strictly meaningless because, as we have shown, one can never know the distribution of g. Any form we happen to choose can be no more than a convention. If IQ is the subject, the weighted sum of test scores does have an empirical distribution and we can determine what it is. In practice such distributions do turn out to be roughly normal. However, this empirical fact has no significance. It is mainly a consequence of the form of the formula we use. Sums, or weighted sums, have a tendency to produce normal distributions and that is all there is to it. In other words, it is an artefact and has no theoretical significance whatsoever. The normality of IQ itself is ensured by the scaling we adopt and is purely for convenience.

(vii)   IQ is a measure of ability to do intelligence tests and very little else[5]

This is one of those statements which, at first sight, seems obviously correct but on closer examination is, quite simply, silly. It is necessarily true that people with high IQ scores are good at doing IQ tests and *vice versa*. That much is tautologous so it tells us nothing. The 'and very little else' is often implied even if it is not spelt out. It is simply false, as though we were to say, 'The passing of the driving test is an indicator of the ability to succeed in driving tests and very little else.' The driving test is specifically designed to test knowledge and skills which a good driver needs to possess. The test items do not necessarily have to be demonstrated at the wheel of a moving car! We have to identify good *indicators* of ability. The point is made even more forcibly if we think of testing the aptitude of prospective pilots. Demonstrating their ability in the cockpit is, simply, not an option. Ability must be tested by finding much simpler tasks which are indicative of good flying skills. An intelligence test is similarly designed. None of these tests is exhaustive. The items included are only a small sample of those that might be used. The point is that they must have been shown to be sufficient to give a good idea of likely performance in a very wide range of real situations.

Howe's twelve 'facts' which are not true[6]

Howe's list looks impressive but the cumulative weight of his case is weakened by the ambiguities which it contains and the tendentious way in which the 'facts' are expressed. The terms 'fact' and 'true' suggest a precision which is lacking in Howe's discussion.

It is particularly important here to bear in mind again that intelligence, IQ and *g* are not synonymous. Much of the force of Howe's critique is dissipated once this simple fact is recognised.

We take them in turn following Howe's numbering.

(1) *Contrary to the assertions of so-called 'experts' on intelligence, it is not true that different racial groups are genetically different in intelligence. Research findings point to an absence of any genetic differences between races that have direct effects upon a person's IQ score.*

There are certainly differences between racial groups in *average* scores obtained in IQ tests. The point at issue is whether any part of that average difference can be attributed to the genetic make up of the races. This is a very difficult question to answer, because race is confounded with so many other factors whose effects it is almost impossible to disentangle. This fact is reflected in Howe's judicious use of the phrase 'direct effects'. It is, nevertheless, confusing for Howe to raise the question in terms of intelligence and then to answer it in terms of IQ.

(2) *It is not true that a young person's intelligence cannot be changed. There is abundant evidence that the intelligence levels of children increase substantially when circumstances are favourable. There are no solid reasons for believing that the skills which are assessed in an IQ test are harder to change than other abilities children acquire.*

This, again, mixes up intelligence and IQ. It claims that intelligence can be changed. It claims that 'intelligence levels' can be increased substantially and that the skills assessed in an IQ test are no harder to change than other abilities. IQ levels can certainly be changed but this does not imply a change in any underlying (innate) ability, like g, of which IQ is only an indicator.

(3) *It is not true that men and women with low intelligence levels are incapable of impressive mental achievements. There are numerous instances of people with low IQs succeeding at difficult problems that demand complex thinking.*

The multidimensional character of 'intelligence' does not preclude those with 'lower intelligence' (Howe probably means low IQ) succeeding with difficult problems, especially if they call on particular mental skills which do not figure prominently in measures of general intelligence like IQ. Similarly, if Howe were talking about g, it would still be the case that there are many mental tasks which do not 'load heavily' on g in which such a person could excel. (The rather convoluted nature of this response illustrates just how careful one must be in distinguishing what one is talking about!) Properly expressed, this objection is true, but does nothing to diminish the value of intelligence testing.

(4) *Genetic influences do not affect people's intelligence directly, except in rare cases involving specific deficits. There is no such thing as a 'gene for intelligence'. Genes affect intelligence indirectly, but in ways that are not inevitable and depend upon other influences being present.*

There is certainly no such thing as a 'gene for intelligence'. I am not aware that any reputable scientist believes that there is, so this 'fact' is in the nature of an 'Aunt Sally'. Many genes are involved but it is going beyond the evidence to suggest that genetic influences do not affect people's intelligence directly. It is more accurate to say that genetic effects are affected by interactions with one another and with environmental factors.

(5) *It is wrong to assume that intelligence can be measured in the way that qualities such as weight and height are measured: it cannot. The belief that IQ tests provide measures of inherent mental capacities has led to unrealistic expectations of what mental testing can achieve.*

Howe is right to point out that intelligence cannot be measured in the same way as height and weight. One of the main objects of this book has been to explain why this is so. Again, it is not clear who has proclaimed this as a 'truth'. It may well be that the belief that IQ tests measure inherent mental capacities has led to unrealistic expectations, but that does not alter the fact they do provide a measure of mental capacity notwithstanding the fact that they are influenced by other things as well.

(6) *IQ scores are only weak predictors of educational or vocational success in individual people. In many cases other kinds of information yield more accurate estimates about a person's future performance.*

This is actually a comment on the usefulness of IQ scores, not on their validity as measures of mental ability. The matter of whether IQ scores are only weak predictors of educational or vocational success, depends on what you mean by 'only weak'. Even where this is a defensible statement we may not be able, in practice, to identify or access the 'other kinds of information'. The advantage of a score like an IQ is that it is available for use in a wide range of circumstances, even though there may be better alternatives available in particular cases.

(7) *Even when IQ scores do predict a person's success at reaching future goals, that is often only because IQ is correlated with other influences that are better predictors, such as education and family background.*

The force of (6) is diminished by the fact that Howe allows in (7) that there are cases where IQ is, in fact, a good predictor. However he claims, in effect, that in such cases IQ is confounded with environmental factors which are often 'really' responsible for its apparent predictive value. We have shown that it may be impossible to disentangle the effects of separate covarying factors and, when this happens, there is no means of apportioning their combined effect between the factors. To claim that such things as family background and education must take precedence in this apportioning exercise is not an empirical argument. In any case, there is empirical evidence for the separate effect of IQ.

(8) *An IQ test score is no more than an indication of someone's performance at a range of mental tasks. The implication that there is just one all-important dimension of intelligence is wrong and unhelpful. Other kinds of intelligence can be equally crucial.*

This is a variant of (vii) above. It is true, by definition, that an IQ test score or a *g*-score is an indication of someone's performance at a range of mental tasks. To say that it is 'no more' than that is absurd – a point we have already made using the 'driving test' example. It is neither wrong nor unhelpful to regard *g*, if that is what Howe was thinking of, as a major dimension of intelligence: *g* is a better measure of that major dimension but that does not rule out IQ altogether. It would be foolish to regard either IQ or *g* as 'all-important'.

(9) *There is no single process or mechanism of the brain that causes people to be more or less intelligent. The belief in a quality of intelligence that provides the driving force making people intelligent is mistaken. An IQ score is merely an indication of a person's mental capabilities: it does not explain them.*

It is difficult to be certain exactly what the 'fact' is, which is being denied. The statement seems to be denying that there is something in the brain which results in high or low IQ scores. There is little precise knowledge of how what goes on in the brain relates to IQ scores but it is almost certainly true that it is not a single process. In the present state of knowledge it goes far beyond the evidence (and contrary to some) to assert that no explanation is to be found in the brain. It seems inconceivable that the role of the brain is entirely neutral in this sole matter when it is known to be central to virtually all other human characteristics. Howe is correct in asserting that IQ is only an indicator and it certainly cannot 'explain' itself.

(10) *The average intelligence levels of nations do not stay constant. There have been large changes from one generation to another, and big improvements in some minority groups.*

Average levels of test scores of nations certainly do not stay constant, as the Flynn effect testifies. Whether or not the same is also true of more fundamental characteristics, such as *g* is, strictly, unknowable. One day it may be possible to say whether brain characteristics affecting *g* change over the generations.

(11) *At the highest levels of creative achievement, having an exceptionally high IQ makes little or no difference. Other factors, including being strongly committed and highly motivated, are much more important.*

This is almost the converse of (3) and similar arguments apply. This statement almost amounts to saying that in groups in which IQ varies very little (such as among those who are exceptionally able) other factors will be behind variations in performance. This is a truism that hardly needs stating and it is almost irrelevant to the general argument. Arguments about extremes are very slippery. No one would deny that commitment and motivation are necessary for *achievement* at the highest level.

(12) *Early experiences and opportunities exert a big influence on intelligence levels. Parents and others can do much to help a child to gain the mental skills associated with high IQ scores.*

There is truth in this if the statements are interpreted at face value as referring to IQ. There is no evidence for their truth if one is talking about *g*.

The truth or falsity of the twelve 'facts' seems less clear cut after a detailed analysis of what they actually say. They contain some important truths together with some half-truths and a few errors. Nothing they assert or deny affects the validity of the general approach to measuring intelligence set out in this book. Their critical tone was, doubtless, calculated to cast a shadow over the whole intelligence testing enterprise. They have certainly provided the opportunity for clarification but no serious damage has been done.

Science and pseudo-science

At the outset, we said that one of our objectives was to separate the science from the ideology. Ideology is concerned with what people believe to be the case on the basis of their general world view. Often, this will arise from a set of values whose origin may be obscure but which are rarely based on empirical observation. Science, on the other hand, is concerned with the disciplined analysis of what the world tells us about itself through empirical observation. It is concerned with how things really are, so far as the senses can reveal them. Scientific method has proved to be a powerful tool which has transformed the way we think about the world. However it is not a sure road to universal truth, especially in the realm of social science – that is, when people are brought into the picture. The subjective and the objective then become inextricably entangled.

Social science is much more difficult than natural science because the systems studied involve vast numbers of interacting and covarying variables, over most of which we have no control. For the most part we can only observe what happens, rather than experiment, and so we are denied the most potent tool in the natural scientist's armoury. Even such a basic thing as measurement becomes a major task in itself as this book amply demonstrates.

It is tempting to brand social science as pseudo-science because it must inevitably fail to deliver firmly established results on the scale hoped for. Yet the paraphernalia of data and the sophisticated analyses which it uses have a distinctly scientific air about them: in a sense, social science thereby borrows an unearned prestige from natural science. The temptation to go beyond the data is almost overwhelming. Even so, Howe's 'truths' were full of qualifications like, 'point to', 'substantially', 'favourable', 'no solid reasons', 'except in rare cases', 'weak predictions', 'often' and 'some'. Almost any conclusion derived from social science risks death by a thousand qualifications. Science becomes pseudo-science when it goes beyond the evidence. Statistics is part of the method of science and its role is, partly, to keep the enterprise within the bounds of what is scientifically defensible.

It is a pity that so much of what has passed for scientific method in this field is outdated, and sometimes wrong. The general plausibility of the conclusions presented by writers often owes more to the author's facility with words than to the accuracy of what those words are intended to convey. Much of the confusion, as we have seen, results from an inadequate conceptual framework. A suitable framework already exists in the world of latent variable modelling and this book provides a non-technical introduction to it.

It is this framework which enables us to answer the kind of question posed in chapter 1 about the usefulness of the whole enterprise. The latent variable model certainly provides an economical and structured way of thinking about intelligence. In particular, it removes the obscurity and ambiguity surrounding indices like IQ. In retrospect, it would have been more appropriate to approach some of the questions from the other end. Rather than ask, for example, what we can do now that was impossible before, it might have been better to note what would now be better avoided. The low level of measurement achievable and the multidimensionality of IQ, for example, argues for building less, rather than more, on this fragile foundation. Most important of all, perhaps, the limitation of measures based on mental tests helps us to see that the way forward lies with brain-based measures permitting a higher level of measurement.

The volume of research on measuring intelligence is enormous but if, after sifting through it with a critical eye, the results seem meagre, this is only to be expected. It is the way the world is and we must learn to understand why that is so and learn to live with it. Nevertheless, intelligence is one of the most fundamental human characteristics and, in spite of everything, its quantitative investigation is one of the great achievements of the social sciences.

Notes

I THE GREAT INTELLIGENCE DEBATE: SCIENCE OR IDEOLOGY?

1 Herrnstein and Murray 1994.
2 The first edition of his *Hereditary Genius, an Inquiry into its Laws and Consequences* appeared in 1869; the second edition in 1892. In the preface to the second edition Galton expressed his regret at his original choice of title. In retrospect he thought that *Hereditary Ability* would have been better.
3 *Measured Lies* (Kincheloe, Steinberg and Gresson, eds. 1996). *Inequality by Design, Cracking the Bell Curve Myth* (Fischer *et al.* 1996) and *The Bell Curve Wars, Race, Intelligence and the Future of America* (Fraser, ed. 1995) are not the only book-length assaults on *The Bell Curve* but, together, they convey something of the heat of the battle. Jacoby and Glauberman (1995) is a useful source of background material.
4 The trigger for much of the furore was a lengthy article which Arthur Jensen was invited to write (Jensen 1969). It has been reprinted several times (for details of which see Miele 2002, p. 197). It asked the question 'How much can we boost IQ and scholastic achievement?' Jensen's answer was that efforts to do this had achieved very little.
5 The first edition of Gould (1996) appeared in 1981 but a revised and expanded edition followed in 1996. This allowed Gould to respond to *The Bell Curve*. Gould's response received a number of critical reviews from researchers in the field, including a particularly hostile review by J. Philippe Rushton (Rushton 1997) but these do not seem to have dented its popular appeal.
6 The three books noted here (Richardson 1999, Howe 1997 and Rose 1997) are all unsympathetic to IQ testing and their views have been repeated in articles elsewhere. Rose was a joint author of another oft-quoted earlier book (Rose, Lewontin and Kamin, 1984).
7 Gardner 1993, pp. 60–1. This is the tenth anniversary edition of a book which first appeared in 1983.
8 Sternberg 1982.
9 One of the most frequently cited definitions occurs as a pre-amble to a statement, signed by fifty behavioural scientists, on the meaning and measurement of intelligence which appeared in the *Wall Street Journal* (13 December, 1994). It says:

> Intelligence is a very general mental capability that, among other things, involves the ability to reason, plan, solve problems, think abstractly, comprehend complex ideas, learn quickly and learn from experience. It is not merely book learning, a narrow academic skill, or test-taking smarts. Rather, it reflects a broader and deeper capability for comprehending our surroundings – 'catching on', 'making sense' of things, or 'figuring out', what to do.

153

10 It is commonplace for those unsympathetic to intelligence testing to assume an attitude of lofty detachment when commenting on the items used in tests. One recent commentator, referring to a BBC television programme called *Test the Nation*, said, 'Puzzle-solving of the type favoured by these tests reveals nothing but a dogged attachment to the processes of a full logic, the mark of any true nerd. Any useful form of brightness, imagination and wit, the ability to understand and appreciate light and shade and nuance – in other words, the very qualities which, if deployed in IQ tests, will have you down among the dead men at the bottom of the class' (Terence Blacker, *The Independent* 7 May 2002). We shall meet a similar utterance by David Best later (see note 16, below). Such writers do not seem to be aware that they are making empirically testable assertions which have been tested!

11 This, circular, definition can be traced back at least as far as E. G. Boring's article in *New Republic*, 1923 (vol. 35, pp. 35–7). See note at end of Carroll's chapter in Sternberg 1982 (p. 109).

12 Howe 1997.

13 Charles E. Spearman (1863–1945), who spent his academic career at University College London (1907–31), is one of the giants of the story of intelligence testing. Details of his career and achievements can be found in the article by Jensen (Jensen 2000, pp. 93–111). A review of Spearman's contributions to the development of factor analysis is given in Bartholomew 1995.

14 See Jensen 1998, especially, on this point, pp. xi and xii of the preface and pp. 46–48.

15 Rose 1997.

16 *Times Higher Educational Supplement*, 3 January 2002, p. 14.

17 Rose 1997, p. 284.

18 Alfred Binet (1857–1911) gave his name (along with his co-worker Théodore Simon) to tests intended to identify children who would benefit from extra tuition. There is a good deal of material in Zenderland 1998 about his work and his relationship with Spearman and other pioneers.

19 See, especially, the list of contributors to Kincheloe *et al.* (1996) – one of the least temperate contributions.

20 H. J. Eysenck was among the first and most enduring authors in this field with the titles *Test Your IQ* and *Check Your Own IQ*. A more recent entry is *Test Your IQ* by A. W. Munzert and K. Munzert. At the time of writing one among many tests is available at www.personaltest.co.uk. A good introductory account of the Wechsler tests and Raven's matrices is given in Mackintosh 1998, pp. 28–38.

2 ORIGINS

Although this chapter is historical, it makes no pretence to be a history. Some of the books listed in the References are, of course, part of the history of intelligence testing; for example, Galton 1892 and Terman 1916. Matarazzo 1972 provides a great deal of background material about the construction of scales, Fancher 1985 focuses on many of the key individuals in the history of intelligence testing and Brody 1992 summarises much of the pioneering work. Deary 2000, especially in chapters 2 and 3, gives interesting historical information going back to the sixteenth century. However, much of the early material, though concerned with individual differences, is not about measurement as such.

1 Spearman's fundamental paper (Spearman 1904, pp. 201–93) marks the birth of factor analysis. The details of the methodology are somewhat obscure and it is still not entirely clear how Spearman carried out his calculations. Nevertheless, the essential ideas are here and, given that multivariate statistical methods as we know them today did not exist, it was highly original. Lovie and Lovie 1996 contains much biographical information on Spearman including his work on 'general intelligence'. In a sense, Spearman's 'last' word is in Spearman and Jones 1950. His main book-length contribution is Spearman 1927b.

2 Fancher (1985) covers many of the pioneers, including Wechsler, Terman, Binet and Spearman. He records Wechsler's brief association with Spearman and also notes that Spearman himself knew of Binet's tests, with which he was not greatly impressed. Binet, for his part, reviewed Spearman's fundamental paper critically.

3 Wilhelm Stern is usually credited with first using the quotient of mental and chronological age. His reasons had to do with what was then called feeblemindedness and its rate of development. Terman multiplied the quotient by 100 and coined the term IQ.

4 David Wechsler (1896–1981) constructed, and made available on a commercial basis, a number of IQ tests which bear his name. The first edition of his book *The Measurement of Adult Intelligence* appeared in 1939. A fifth edition, written by J. D. Matarazzo, appeared under a slightly different title (Matarazzo 1972). The information about Wechsler's work given here comes mainly from that source.

5 I am not aware that this correspondence has been noted before but it may be seen easily by considering a diagram of 'score' plotted against 'age'. The postulated relationship is a straight line through the origin.

6 Galton (see also chapter 1, note 2) introduced the correlation coefficient and it was Karl Pearson's 'biometrical school' at University College London, which developed the theory of correlation and gave it wide currency. Early studies included the relationship between the heights of fathers and sons, which are positively correlated.

7 His explanation of how he decided to tackle the problem of exposition begins on p. 47 of Gould 1996. The explanation itself begins on p. 269.

8 Correlations cannot always be taken at face value. Sometimes they are based on very small numbers and are thus intrinsically imprecise. Sometimes they are based on highly selected information. For example, it is sometimes remarked that the correlation between entry grade to university and exit grade at graduation is surprisingly low. However, only those with high grades are admitted in the first place and the correlation depends on the cut-off point. The more highly selected the entrants the lower, in general, will be the correlations. Thirdly, the variables we seek to correlate may be observed with error because of an imprecise measuring instrument. This blurs (or 'attenuates') the correlation, making it smaller than it would otherwise be.

The elucidation of these matters is not necessary for our present purposes, but the reader should be aware of such complications, especially as well-meant attempts to correct for such distortions are seen, by some critics, as obfuscation rather than clarification.

9 The story was set out in a biography of Burt (Hearnshaw 1979). Hearnshaw had been commissioned to write the biography by Burt's sister, Dr Marian Burt. In the course of his work he became convinced that allegations that Burt had fabricated data

and invented collaborators were true. Since then the waters have become somewhat muddied. A more recent treatment of the whole issue may be found in Mackintosh 1995.

10 The extent of Spearman's involvement in the theoretical side of Burt's work is another fascinating historical by-way investigated by Lovie and Lovie 1993.

11 See Thurstone's books on multiple factor analysis (Thurstone 1935 and 1947). The second is, essentially, a heavily revised version of the first.

Thurstone named nine factors: space, verbal comprehension, word fluency, number facility, induction, perceptual speed, deduction, rote memory and reasoning. Some were regarded as more permanent than others (see Sternberg 1982, p. 70).

12 Thomson's book *The Factorial Analysis of Human Ability* first appeared in 1939 and continued into a fourth edition in 1951. Although now of historical interest only, it has a more 'modern' flavour than its contemporaries (Thomson 1951).

13 Zenderland 1998.

14 Lawley and Maxwell 1963. The more usually quoted, second edition, appeared in 1971. Prior to the Second World War, there was very little interest among statisticians in factor analysis. Before Lawley and Maxwell's groundbreaking book, Maurice Bartlett was almost the only statistician of note to publish in this area.

15 Lazarsfeld and Henry 1968.

3 THE END OF IQ?

1 In the case of 'quality' the following quotation illustrates the point nicely.

> Quality . . . you know what it is, yet you don't know what it is. But that's self-contradictory. But some things *are* better than others, that is, they have more quality. But when you try to say what quality is, apart from the things that have it, it all goes *poof!* There's nothing to talk about. But if you can't say what quality is, how do you know what it is, or how do you know that it even exists? If no one knows what it is, then for all practical purposes it doesn't exist at all. But for all practical purposes it really *does* exist. What else are the grades based on? Why else would people pay fortunes for some things and throw others in the trash pile? Obviously some things are better than others . . . but what's the 'betterness'? . . . So round and round you go, spinning mental wheels and nowhere finding anyplace to get traction. What the hell is quality? What *is* it? (Pirsig 1991, p. 187)

My own approach to social measurement is set out in Bartholomew 1996.

2 The 'Terman tradition' is shorthand for the approach to intelligence testing expounded in Terman 1916, and based upon the Stanford revision of the Binet–Simon intelligence scale.

3 See, for example, Rose 1997, p. 287.

4 Rose 1997 is another example; see bottom of page 285 of that book.

5 The pioneers were well aware that one could not start with a precise and agreed definition of intelligence. See, for example, the discussion of the point in Terman 1916, p. 44.

6 There are, in fact, several such scales which have gone through many revisions. The Wechsler Adult Intelligence Scale (WAIS) is the principal scale but there is also the Wechsler Intelligence Scale for Children (WISC) and the Wechsler–Bellvue I and II scales (W–BI and W–BII). See, for example, Matarazzo 1972.

4 FIRST STEPS TO *g*

1 When considering size and shape as familiar examples of collective properties, it is instructive to consult a dictionary. For example, the *Shorter Oxford Dictionary* gives the relevant definition of 'shape' as 'that quality of a material object which depends on constant relations of position and proportionate distance among all the points composing its outline or its external surface'. It goes on to note the usage in relation to the appearance of the human body.

   In the case of 'size', the dictionary merely offers a set of synonyms: magnitude, bulk, bigness or dimensions of anything. The 'dimensions of anything' conveys the sense of 'collective value'.

2 Having noted above that the volume of a brick (which is close to what we mean by its size) is obtained by multiplication, it may seem perverse to speak of 'adding up' as the characteristic way of combining measurements. The two operations are not so far removed, as those who recall that the product of a set of numbers can be obtained by adding up their logarithms will recognise. For our present purpose, it is sufficient to note that we are only talking about combining numbers in some relevant way.

3 This encounter takes place in chapter 6 of *Alice in Wonderland*. Actually, the smile is a 'grin' in the original story but 'smile' suits our purpose better.

4 *Construct* is a term which is widely used in the field of social measurement for what we are here referring to as a collective property. It is a mental construction and it will often be measured by combining relevant indicators into some kind of index. It is, therefore, much the same as a 'collective property'. The latter term puts greater emphasis, perhaps, on the elements from which the construction is made.

5 SECOND STEPS TO *g*

1 See note 4 of chapter 4. The question is treated again in chapter 13 in relation to the claims of Gould that intelligence is not a 'thing'; a reference is given there to Karl Popper's three 'worlds'.

2 This is a slight over-simplification. The boundaries will not usually be fixed, as illustrated, but fuzzy. This reflects the fact that the probability of a deviation from the centre falls off as we move away from it. This does not affect the essence of the argument.

3 S. S. Stevens (Stevens 1946) is usually credited with introducing the notion of levels of measurement. He classified them as *nominal, ordinal, interval* and *ratio*. The nominal level can hardly be described as measurement. It refers to the situation where individuals can only be placed in un-ordered categories, such as 'country of birth'. The ordinal level, which applies to *g*, is where individuals can be ranked only.

4 He said, for example, 'such a general and quantitative factor it was said, might be conceived in an infinitude of different ways . . . But a readily intelligible hypothesis was suggested to be derivable from physiology. The factor was taken, pending further information, to consist in something of the nature of an "energy" or "power" which serves in common the whole cortex (or possibly, even, the whole nervous system)' (Spearman 1927a, p. 5).

5 A recent treatment of the link between performance in tests and the brain is given in Deary 2000. Its subtitle 'From psychometrics to the brain' expresses perfectly the thrust of its argument. It deals with a wider range of brain characteristics than those mentioned here, in particular, with brain metabolism.

6 EXTRACTING *g*

1 This way of approaching factor analysis has been advocated by the author for many years. The idea was first worked out in the paper 'The foundations of factor analysis' (Bartholomew 1984) and was subsequently used as the basis of the general treatment of latent variable models (Bartholomew and Knott 1999). Reference to the 1984 paper was, unaccountably, omitted from both Bartholomew and Knott 1999 and Bartholomew 1996.

   Readers familiar with latent structure analysis will recognise the principle expounded in this paragraph as very close to the 'assumption of local independence' (or 'conditional independence') which is central to that topic. In fact, it would be better described as a 'postulate' because it is not an assumption in the usual sense. It is actually a statement of what it means to have a set of 'correlations' explained by their dependence on a latent variable. The same postulate is also part of the specification of the standard factor analysis model though it never seems to have attracted the same attention. Another way of looking at what we are doing here is to say that we are looking for some quantity, calculated from the data, which will mirror the role of the latent variable as closely as possible. If we can find such a quantity it must be similar to the latent variable and hence may serve as a substitute for it.

2 Statisticians, who are familiar with sufficiency, may detect that, in technical language, the sufficient statistic might depend on unknown parameters of the model. We get round this problem by treating any such unknowns as known, and then substituting estimates. This complication can be ignored for present purposes.

3 The reference to regression may ring bells with some readers which will make this section clearer. Essentially we are supposing that each indicator can be regressed on the latent variables. We thus have a set of regression equations (one for each indicator). The unusual feature is that none of the regressor variables (the latent variables) are known. This is why fitting the model is more complicated than standard regression analysis.

4 It is not easy to appreciate the pioneering character of this small book. As its title indicates, it aimed to bring factor analysis into the statistical fold. One of its authors (Maxwell), at least, felt that the book had not been well received but it was reprinted in 1967 and a second edition appeared in 1971.

5 There is an enormous literature on item response theory. A useful point of entry is van der Linden and Hambleton 1997. More general methods for polytomous data and more than one latent variable will be found in Bartholomew *et al.* 2002.

6 See Bartholomew and Knott 1999, chapter 2.

7 FACTOR ANALYSIS OR PRINCIPAL COMPONENTS ANALYSIS?

1 A non-technical account of principal components analysis with examples will be found in Bartholomew *et al.* 2002, chapter 5. The difference between principal components analysis and factor analysis can be characterised in various ways. One way is in terms of how they decompose the total variation. PCA decomposes the whole variance whereas FA decomposes only that part which is due to the common factors. Again, factor analysis is often said (not entirely accurately) to 'explain' the covariances (or correlations) among the variables whereas PCA 'explains' the variance. It is nearer to the distinction made here to say that PCA is a special, or limiting, case of factor

analysis arrived at when the number of factors is equal to the number of variables and when the residual variance is zero. Here we have regarded factor analysis as a 'model-based' method as opposed to PCA which is a descriptive procedure which can be applied to any set of numbers regardless of how they have been generated.

2 Principal components analyses are sometimes carried out using pseudo-correlation coefficients derived from categorical variables. This is unnecessary as there are better ways of dealing with the problem.

3 More information on this point will be found in Bartholomew *et al.* 2002, section 6.10 (see above in note 1).

4 Jensen 1998. See, especially, note 2 beginning on page 95. Actually, Jensen recognises the difference between factor analysis and PCA and regards the latter more in the nature of an approximation to the former. A rather different use of PCA is mentioned by Jensen in Miele 2002, pp. 120–1.

5 Mackintosh 1998. See chapter 6, especially p. 216.

6 Hotelling 1933.

7 The difference between PCA and PAF lies in the technicalities of how they treat the table (matrix) of correlations. PAF fits a factor model whereas PCA does not.

8 ONE INTELLIGENCE OR MANY?

1 See, for example, Golman 1996. Since 1996 there has been a flow of further books on the topic by the same author and others.

2 See Zohar and Marshall 2001. Although spiritual intelligence was later on the scene than emotional intelligence, there are signs of more to come.

3 Gardner 1993, given in the list of references, is the tenth anniversary edition of the book which first appeared in 1983. The anniversary edition has a new introduction by the author. There is a more recent collection of essays by the same author (Gardner 2001).

4 The triarchic theory is set out in Sternberg 1985. Sternberg does not deny the importance of g but argues that it gives too limited a view of what is a complex phenomenon.

5 The reference is to Edward Lee Thorndike (1874–1949) whose main book in this field was *The Measurement of Intelligence* (Thorndike 1927).

6 A recent, and sophisticated, treatment of this approach is given in Carroll's chapter 6 in Devlin *et al.* 1997. Carroll 1993 is a major study of the factor analytic approach in this field. See also note 8 below.

7 Matarazzo 1972.

8 Hierarchical factor analysis is closely related to something known as covariance structure analysis. This generalises factor analysis by allowing there to be relationships among the latent variables. In the intelligence testing context this allows one to specify a model in which, for example, group factors are related to one or more factors at a deeper level. The basic idea goes back to Jöreskog 1970, and is best known today through the software packages which implement the method. Prominent among these is LISREL which stems directly from Jöreskog's pioneering work.

LISREL and similar packages are widely used in social science research but their use in intelligence testing is problematic. The reasons for this are common to other applications and are set out in Bartholomew and Knott 1999, section 8.15. As claimed in the text, hierarchical models seem to offer little in the search for g.

9 This result depends on variation being measured by sums of squares – or variances. In the case of the factor model we are then able to identify the contribution which each factor makes.

10 Readers familiar with the way that rotation is used in factor analysis may be slightly puzzled by the discussion in this section. The usual purpose of rotation is to facilitate interpretation by searching for what is known as 'simple structure'. The software available in the standard packages is designed specifically for this purpose. The aim is to identify groups of variables which have a lot in common and so can be considered as a group. Thus, for example, items concerned with numeracy might 'go together' in this way as would those concerned with literacy.

This procedure may also be the first step to identifying higher order factors and thus is a first step to g. Carroll's approach, mentioned in note 6 above, is essentially along these lines. We have suggested a more direct route to g by seeking a rotation which yields a dominant factor at the first stage. In practice most packages yield something very close to a dominant factor directly without the need for further rotation. There is room for debate about which is the better way to uncover g but the results are similar and the distinction need not detain us here. The important point is that there are many ways of describing the factor space and our interpretation must take account of that fact.

11 Gardner 1993. See note 3 above.

12 See Jensen 1998, pp. 128–32.

13 Raymond B. Cattell (1905–98) began his career as a student of Spearman. His major book on factor analysis is *The Scientific Use of Factor Analysis in Behavioural and Life Sciences* 1978. This is a comprehensive, if somewhat idiosyncratic, treatment written towards the end of the author's career. It emphasises the 'scientific' as opposed to the mathematical or statistical approaches and may be regarded as an example of the limitations of the approach of the pre-modern era.

14 J. P. Guilford's (1897–1987) work is briefly discussed in Jensen 1998, pp. 115–17. Guilford's book *The Nature of Human Intelligence* 1967 may be consulted for further information about his 'structure of intellect' ideas.

9 THE BELL CURVE: FACTS, FALLACIES AND SPECULATIONS

1 Herrnstein and Murray 1994. It is odd that in a book entitled *The Bell Curve*, the distribution itself plays a minor role. It does not appear in the Introduction, which contains a historical review, and it is not mentioned in the 'six conclusions' that are now 'beyond significant technical dispute' on pp. 23 and 24. The first mention is on p. 44 where, in relation to the *normal distribution*, it is remarked that 'Most mental tests are designed to produce normal distributions.'

2 Matarazzo 1972. See pp. 102–4, pp. 123–6 and, especially, the references to his figures 10.2 and 10.3 in figure 5.1.

3 Zenderland 1998 makes the interesting observation that early workers seem to have regarded the approximate normality of, for example, the army alpha test scores, as establishing its 'scientific basis'. She says (p. 293), 'Far more important, they argued, was that the scores still fell roughly along a bell curve, for such a curve, these psychologists believed, offered the most convincing proof of their scientific validity.' In reality all that it did was to show that the question they should have been asking was: why is adding up scores a scientifically defensible procedure? An answer to that question has been given in chapter 6.

4 Almost any text book on statistical theory will give a version of the Central Limit Theorem but it is rare, in elementary treatments, to find a statement general enough to cover our needs here.

5 There appears to be a shift of interest away from the purely statistical or psychometric approaches to measuring intelligence and towards one based on neuroscience. Deary 2000 represents this trend, explicitly linking psychometrics and the brain.

6 See, for example, the Postscript on page 140 of Gould 1996. It may be that if Gould had not excluded all new work which had appeared in the fifteen years since the first edition, he might have modified this conclusion.

7 The capacity for processing information is increasingly seen as an important component of intelligence. On this see Deary 2000 and Jensen 1998, chapter 8.

8 It is, in fact, possible to construct a mixture (of an infinite number of normal distributions) which is itself normal, but this does not detract from the point being made here.

9 A rectangular distribution, of course, looks the same both ways up! The point here is that we put the bases of the two distributions in close proximity so that the 'stretching' and 'squeezing' is more obvious.

10 WHAT IS *g*?

1 The standard, but somewhat dated, reference is Lazarsfeld and Henry 1968. A modern treatment of many of the models will be found in Bartholomew and Knott 1999.

2 For an example of the use of latent class models in the industrial relations field see Wood and de Menezes 1998.

3 To the best of my knowledge, this was first noted in Bartholomew 1987, but it has been more fully investigated in Molenaar and von Eye 1994.

4 The reason for this being regarded as a 'problem' is one of the most curious in the history of the subject. Viewed from a modern perspective, there is no real problem at all. It is a perfect example of how important it is to specify, precisely and clearly, the model with which one is working. Readers with the interest and patience to pursue the matter might consult the debate which took place in the journal *Multivariate Behavioral Research*. See Maraun 1996.

5 The scores are not usually described as expected values in the standard software. Two commonly used types of score are known as *regression* scores and *Bartlett* scores. In the case of the linear factor model these are equivalent to the expected values.

11 ARE SOME GROUPS MORE INTELLIGENT THAN OTHERS?

1 For example, the statement 'Moreover, African Americans as a group are permanently set at a lower level of intelligence than Whites' in Kincheloe *et al.* 1996, p. 162 would encourage the view among the statistically unsophisticated that all in one group were below all of the other in intelligence.

2 An exception is Jensen 1998, pp. 536–7.

3 Rose 1997, pp. 286–7 and Richardson 1999, p. 40.

4 See Flynn 1984, 1987 and 1999 and Neisser 1998. Flynn's more recent work, with Dickens, showing how massive changes in IQ might occur over time is discussed in chapter 12. See note 8 of that chapter.

5 As reported in 'Passive smoking dents children's IQ', *New Scientist*, 11 May 2002.

6 A book-length treatment of this study is given in Bennett 1976 but the data have been re-analysed many times since. A notable example is Aitkin *et al.* 1981.

7 We have discussed group differences in the important, but narrow, context of black/white differences in the USA. These groups are well defined and have been the subject of much research and debate. However, from a scientific point of view, it makes more sense to compare groups formed on the basis of genetic similarity. It would be more informative to ask whether such groups differed in average mental ability. This is an immensely difficult area and some of the complexities involved emerged in the discussion between Jensen and Miele in chapter 4 of Miele 2002.

8 The problem here is that factor scores, and *g*-scores in particular, are not simply weighted averages of test scores. The weight to be given to each item has to be estimated from the test scores themselves. What the implications might be in the present context remains to be investigated.

9 This conclusion is expressed with caution, because it is not possible here to do justice to the full complexities of the argument. The reader who wishes to pursue the matter might begin with Brody 1992, chapter 10, and Jensen 1998, chapters 11 and 12.

12 IS INTELLIGENCE INHERITED?

1 This, at least, appears to be the interpretation of his remark 'There exist no data which should lead a prudent man to accept the hypothesis that IQ scores are in any degree heritable' in Kamin 1974, p. 1. A similar, negatively worded, version of this statement is made on p. 176. This, of course, was said a long time ago and it would not be easy to make the same claim today. Nevertheless, it serves to emphasise the wide range of estimates which have been made.

2 Snyderman and Rothman 1988.

3 Sir Ronald Fisher (1890–1962) achieved distinction as a statistician and as a population geneticist. He has been judged to be the greatest statistician of all time. The analysis of variance, as a way of apportioning total variation to its sources, became a fundamental part of statistical analysis. Its application in genetics is only one example of its use.

4 Devlin *et al.* 1997 is one of the responses to the publication of *The Bell Curve*. It appeared after the first flood of polemical literature and gives a broad, measured and reliable account.

5 They are, in fact, rather dismissive of different ways of measuring heritability. They say, 'Specialists have come up with dozens of procedures for estimating heritability' (p. 106). This seems to imply that the differences between them are unimportant.

6 The value obtained for the index of heritability also depends on the scaling chosen for IQ. Conventionally, IQ is scaled to have a normal distribution and it is from these values that heritability is calculated. However, if we left it untransformed, or transformed it to have another distribution, the heritability would change. Given all the other qualifications with which heritability is hedged about, one more complication may not seem serious. We mention it simply to underline the arbitrariness which lies lurking in unexpected quarters.

7 From a *New Scientist* article 11 May 2002, p. 11. Based on an article by Martine Savard and others in *Geology*, 30, 403.

8 Dickens and Flynn 2001.

9 Thompson *et al.* 2002.

13 FACTS AND FALLACIES

1 A convenient summary of objections will be found in Chapman 1988. Some are mentioned on p. 70 and those raised by Walter Lippmann, writing in *New Republic*, are reproduced on pp. 135–6.

   Marxist criticisms, quoted in Wooldridge 1994, have been expressed on the following lines. 'In particular, intelligence tests and the theory of innate inequality of abilities which underpinned them, served both to justify an unequal social system and to disguise as rational a system of educational selection which was systematically biased towards the middle classes.'

   Some critics have conveyed the impression that the world of intelligence testing is built on sand with few solid achievements to its credit. To counteract this view, the American Psychological Association set up a task force, chaired by U. Neisser, to produce an authoritative statement of what is known and what is unknown about intelligence. Their report was published as Neisser *et al.* 1996. A press release is, at the time of writing, available at www.apa.org/releases/intell.html.

2 Gould 1996. Reference to the alleged fallacies, collectively or individually, is made at many points in the book. See, for example, pp. 27, 48 and 189.

3 Readers who wish to pursue the philosophical side of reification might consult Karl Popper on the subject (Popper and Eccles 1983). He classifies objects as belonging to World 1, World 2 or World 3. Physical objects like bricks and tables belong to World 1. Schubert's Unfinished Symphony – as a product of the human mind – belongs to World 3. IQ, thought of as a measuring instrument, is another World 3 object. Popper argues that World 3 objects are real. He traces this kind of classification back to Plato, who made similar distinctions, but Popper argues that there are important differences between his classification and Plato's.

4 Joyce King (Kincheloe *et al.* 1996, p. 185) is one of those who, in trenchantly denying that the distribution is normal, reveals a profound misunderstanding of the true state of affairs. See also Richardson 1999, pp. 41ff.

5 This is not another way of expressing the tautologous definition of intelligence but a claim that test items measure the wrong thing. The items, it is argued, are too close to 'school knowledge' or are 'paper and pencil' tests far removed from the realities of the real world. As such they fail to capture the richness and depth of truly intelligent behaviour. One finds this view expressed in various forms – for example, in Fischer *et al.* 1996, pp. 40ff.

6 Howe 1997, chapter 10.

ADDITIONAL READING

The literature on intelligence and intelligence testing is vast. Not all of it is concerned with measurement but many of the most significant books relating to measurement have been referred to in the text and are thus included in the References which follow. Among books not referred to and published since 1990, we have added Locurto 1990, Nash 1990, Kline 1991, Anderson 1992, Rushton 1995, Perkins 1995, Sternberg and Grigorenko 1997 and Deary 2001.

References

Aitkin, M., Anderson, D. and Hinde, J. 1981, 'Statistical modelling of data on teaching styles', *Journal of the Royal Statistical Society*, A, 144, 419–48.

Anderson, M. 1992, *Intelligence and Development: A Cognitive Theory*, Oxford: Blackwell.

Bartholomew, D. J. 1984, 'The foundations of factor analysis', *Biometrika*, 71, 221–32.

1995, 'Spearman and the origin and development of factor analysis', *British Journal of Mathematical and Statistical Psychology*, 48, 211–20.

1996, *The Statistical Approach to Social Measurement*, San Diego: Academic Press.

Bartholomew, D. J. and Knott, M. 1999, *Latent Variable Models and Factor Analysis*, London: Arnold.

Bartholomew, D. J., Steele, F., Moustaki, I. and Galbraith, J. I. 2002, *The Analysis and Interpretation of Multivariate Data for Social Science*, London: Chapman and Hall/CRC.

Bennett, H. 1976, *Teaching Styles and Pupil Progress*, London: Open Books.

Brody, N. 1992, *Intelligence*, 2nd edn, New York: Academic Press.

Carroll, J. P. 1982, 'The measurement of intelligence' in Sternberg (ed.) 1982, pp. 29–120.

1993, *Human Cognitive Abilities: A Survey of Factor-Analytic Studies*, Cambridge University Press.

Cattell, R. B. 1978, *The Scientific Use of Factor Analysis in Behavioural and Life Sciences*, New York: Plenum Press.

Chapman, P. D. 1988, *Schools as Sorters: Lewis M. Terman, Applied Psychology and the Intelligence Testing Movement, 1890–1930*, New York and London: New York University Press.

Deary, I. J. 2000, *Looking Down on Human Intelligence: From Psychometrics to the Brain*, Oxford University Press.

2001 *Intelligence: A Very Short Introduction*, Oxford University Press.

Devlin, B., Fienberg, S. E., Resnick, D. P. and Roeder, K. (eds.) 1997, *Intelligence, Genes and Success*, New York: Springer-Verlag.

Dickens, W. T. and Flynn, J. R. 2001, 'Heritability estimates versus large environmental effects: the IQ paradox resolved', *Psychological Review,* 108, 346–69.

Fancher, R. E. 1985, *The Intelligence Men, and the IQ Controversy*, New York and London: Norton, W. W.

Fischer, C. S., Hout, M., Jankowski, M. S., Lucas, S. R., Swidler, S. and Voss, K. 1996, *Inequality by Design: Cracking the Bell Curve Myth*, Princeton University Press.

Flynn, J. R. 1984, 'The mean IQ of Americans: massive gains 1932–1978', *Psychological Bulletin*, 95, 29–51.

1987, 'Massive gains in 14 nations: what IQ tests really measure', *Psychological Bulletin*, 101, 171–91.

1998, 'IQ gains over time: towards finding the causes' in Neisser (ed.) 1998.

1999, 'Searching for justice: the discovery of IQ gains over time', *American Psychologist*, 54, 5–20.

Fraser, S. (ed.) 1995, *The Bell Curve Wars: Race, Intelligence and the Future of America*, New York: Basic Books.

Galton, F. 1892, *Hereditary Genius*, 2nd edn, London: Macmillan.

Gardner, H. 1993, *Frames of Mind: The Theory of Multiple Intelligences*, New York: Basic Books, 10th anniversary edition.

2001, *Intelligence Reframed: Multiple Intelligences for the 21st Century*, New York: Basic Books.

Golman, D. 1996, *Emotional Intelligence: Why it Can Matter More Than IQ*, London: Bloomsbury Paperbacks.

Gould, S. J. 1996, *The Mismeasure of Man*, Harmondsworth, Middlesex: Penguin Books (revised and expanded version of the first edition 1981; New York: Norton).

Guilford, J. P. 1967, *The Nature of Human Intelligence*, New York: McGraw-Hill.

Hearnshaw, L. S. 1979, *Cyril Burt, Psychologist*, London: Hodder and Stoughton.

Herrnstein, R. J. and Murray, C. 1994, *The Bell Curve. Intelligence and Class Structure in American Life*, New York: Free Press Paperbacks.

Hotelling, H. 1933, 'Analysis of complex statistical variables into principal components', *Journal of Educational Psychology*, 24, 417–41, 498–520.

Howe, M. J. A. 1997, *IQ in Question. The Truth about Intelligence*, Thousand Oaks CA: Sage Publications.

Jacoby, R. and Glauberman, N. (eds.) 1995, *The Bell Curve Debate: History, Documents and Opinion*, New York: Random House.

Jensen, A. R. 1969, 'How much can we boost IQ and scholastic achievement?' *Harvard Educational Review*, 39, 1–123.

1998, *The g Factor. The Science of Mental Ability*, Westport, Connecticut and London: Praeger.

2000, 'Charles E. Spearman; the discoverer of *g*' in *Portraits of Pioneers in Psychology*, IV, pp. 93–111, Kimble, G. A. and Wertheimer, M. (eds.) Washington DC: American Psychological Association and Mahwah NJ: Laurence Erlbaum Associates.

Jöreskog, K. G. 1970, 'A general method for analysis of covariance structures', *Biometrika*, 57, 239–51.

Kincheloe, J. L., Steinberg, S. R. and Gressen, A. D. (eds.) 1996, *Measured Lies. The Bell Curve Examined,* New York: St Martin's Press.

Kline, P. 1991, *Intelligence: The Psychometric View*, London and New York: Routledge.

Lawley, D. N. and Maxwell, A. E. 1963, *Factor Analysis as a Statistical Method*, London: Butterworths (2nd edn 1971).

Lazarsfeld, P. and Henry, N. W. 1968, *Latent Structure Analysis*, New York: Houghton Mifflin.

Locurto, C. 1990, *Sense and Nonsense about IQ: The Case for Uniqueness*, New York: Praeger.

Lovie, A. D. and Lovie, P. 1993, 'Charles Spearman, Cyril Burt and the origins of factor analysis', *Journal of the History of the Behavioural Sciences*, 29, 308–21.

1996. 'Charles Edward Spearman, F. R. S. (1863–1945)', *Notes and Records, Royal Society of London*, 50, 75–88.

Mackintosh, N. J. (ed.) 1995, *Cyril Burt: Fraud or Framed?* Oxford University Press.

1998, *IQ and Human Intelligence*, Oxford University Press.

Maraun, M. D. 1996, 'Metaphor taken as math: indeterminacy in the factor analysis model, *Multivariate Behavioral Research*, 31, 517–38.

Matarazzo, J. D. 1972, *Wechsler's Measurement and Appraisal of Adult Intelligence*, 5th edn, New York: Oxford University Press (1st edn by Wechsler, D. 1939, published by Williams and Wilkins, Baltimore, as *The Measurement of Adult Intelligence*).

Miele, F. 2002, *Intelligence, Race and Genetics: Conversations with Arthur R. Jensen*, Boulder, Colorado and Oxford: Westview Books.

Molenaar, P. C. W. and von Eye, A. 1994, 'On the arbitrary nature of latent variables' in von Eye, A. and Clogg, C. C., *Latent Variables Analysis*, Thousand Oaks CA: Sage Publications, pp. 226–42.

Nash, P. 1990, *Intelligence and Realism: A Materialist Critique of IQ*, London: Routledge.

Neisser, U. (ed.) 1998, *The Rising Curve: Long-term Gains in IQ and Related Measures*, Washington DC: American Psychological Association.

Neisser, U. *et al.* 1996, 'Intelligence, knowns and unknowns', *American Psychologist*, 51, 77–101.

Perkins, D. N. 1995, *Outsmarting IQ: The Emerging Science of Learnable Intelligence*, New York: Free Press.

Pirsig, R. M. 1991, *Zen and the Art of Motorcycle Maintenance*, London: Vintage (first published 1974 in Great Britain by the Bodley Head Ltd).

Popper, K. R. and Eccles, J. C. 1983, *The Self and its Brain: An Argument for Interactionism*, London and New York: Routledge and Kegan Paul.

Richardson, K. 1999, *The Making of Intelligence*, London: Weidenfeld and Nicolson; paperback, 2000, London: Phoenix.

Rose, S. 1997, *Lifelines: Biology, Freedom, Determinism*, Harmondsworth, Middlesex: Allen Lane, The Penguin Press.

Rose, S., Lewontin, R. C. and Kamin, L. 1984, *Not in Our Genes*, Harmondsworth, Middlesex: Penguin Books.

Rushton, J. P. 1995, *Race, Evolution and Behaviour*, New Brunswick NJ: Transaction Books.

1997, 'Race, intelligence, and the brain: the errors and omissions of the "revised" edition of S. J. Gould's *The Mismeasure of Man* (1996)', *Personality and Individual Differences*, 23, 169–80.

Sham Pak 1998, *Statistics and Human Genetics*, London: Arnold.

Snyderman, M. and Rothman, S. 1988, *The IQ Controversy, the Media and Public Policy*, New Brunswick NJ: Transaction Books.

Spearman, C. 1904, '"General intelligence" objectively determined and measured', *American Journal of Psychology*, 5, 201–93.

1927a, *The Nature of Intelligence and the Principles of Cognition*, London: Macmillan.

1927b, *The Abilities of Man: Their Nature and Measurement*, London: Macmillan.

Spearman, C. and Jones, L. W. 1950, *Human Ability*, London: Macmillan.

Sternberg, R. J. (ed.) 1982, *Handbook of Human Intelligence*, Cambridge University Press (2nd edn 2000).

1985, *Beyond IQ: A Triarchic New Theory of Human Intelligence*, Cambridge University Press.

Sternberg, R. J. and Grigorenko, E. (eds.) 1997, *Intelligence, Heredity and Environment*, Cambridge University Press.

Stevens, S. S. 1946, 'On the theory of scales of measurement', *Science*, 103, 677–80.

Terman, L. M. 1916, *The Measurement of Intelligence*, Boston: Houghton Mifflin.

Thompson, P., Cannon, T. D., Narr, K. L., van Erp, T., Poutanen, V.-P., Huttunen, M., Lönnqvist, J., Standertskjöld-Nordenstam, C.-G., Kaprio, J., Khaledy, M., Dail, R., Zoumalan, C. I. and Toga, A. W. 2002, 'Genetic influences on brain structure', *Nature Neuroscience Online*, 4, no. 12, 1253–8.

Thomson, G. 1951, *The Factorial Analysis of Human Ability*, 4th edn, London University Press.

Thorndike, E. L. 1927, *The Measurement of Intelligence*, New York: Teachers College.

Thurstone, L. L. 1935, *The Vectors of the Mind*, 4th edn, University of Chicago Press.

1947, *Multiple Factor Analysis*, University of Chicago Press.

van der Linden, W. J. and Hambleton, R. 1997, *Handbook of Modern Item Response Theory*, New York: Springer-Verlag.

Wood, S. J. and de Menezes, L. M. 1998, 'High commitment management in the UK: evidence from the Workplace Industrial Relations Survey and Employers' Manpower Skills Practices Survey', *Human Relations*, 51, 485–515.

Wooldridge, A., 1994, *Measuring the Mind: Education and Psychology in England c. 1860–c. 1990*, Cambridge University Press.

Zenderland, L. 1998, *Measuring Minds, Henry Herbert Goddard and the Origins of American Intelligence Testing*, Cambridge University Press.

Zohar, D. and Marshall, I. 2001, *SQ: The Ultimate Intelligence*, London: Bloomsbury Paperbacks.

Index